i Hebrew™

ulpan·or
Hebrew at the speed of light
SINCE 1995

עִבְרִית בְּכֵיף

פועל - עתיד

רמה ב' ומעלה

Learn Hebrew the Fun Way

iHebrew™ - a series of interactive rapid Hebrew study kits

Hebrew Verbs - Future Tense

Intermediate Level and Up

Orly & Yoel Ganor אוֹרְלִי וְיוֹאֵל גָּנוֹר

Copyright © 1995-2013 by Orly & Yoel Ganor כל הזכויות שמורות
All rights reserved to Orly and Yoel Ganor
No part of this book may be reproduced or transmitted in any form or by any means without written permission from Orly and Yoel Ganor.

Catalogue No. VER-FT-2013-2S-RH6   Ulpan-Or: www.ulpanor.com
ISBN 978-965-7573-18-1

Copyrighted and owned by Ulpan-Or. Any usage without express permission from Ulpan-Or is prohibited. RH6
כל הזכויות שמורות לאולפן-אור. כל שימוש, העתקה והפצה אסורים.

Welcome

Shalom from Yoel and Orly, the developers of a unique language learning methodology **RLA** (***R**apid **L**anguage **A**cquisition*) and founders of Ulpan-Or, where students learn Hebrew at the speed of light.

Welcome to "Hebrew Verbs – Future Tense" study kit, which is part of our *i*Hebrew™ comprehensive program designed for all levels and ages.

"Hebrew Verbs – Future Tense" is presented to you after two decades of research. Being engaged in this research, we have developed our unique RLA – Rapid Language Acquisition method, with the aim of helping people overcome their fear of Hebrew grammar.

We designed this study kit with the idea of simplifying the Hebrew verb structure to let you enjoy the beauty and the intrinsic musical qualities of Hebrew grammar.

This book contains all major Hebrew verb groups (Binyanim) in the future tense.

We'll be delighted to help you with your studies and would also appreciate getting any comments or remarks.

Please feel free to contact us at: office@ulpanor.com

With very best wishes,

Orly & Yoel

Table of Contents

Ulpan-Or *i*Hebrew™ Study Kit Series	……………………	Pg. 5
Study instructions	…………………………………………	Pg. 8
General Introduction	………………………………………..	Pg. 10
Verb Groups – Introduction	………………………………..	Pg. 12
Time Words – Future Tense	………………………………..	Pg. 14
General Structure of the Future Tense	……………………..	Pg. 16
Imperative Form	……………………………………………	Pg. 18
Future Tense – Binyan Hif'eel	……………………………..	Pg. 21
Future Tense – Binyan Hitpa'el	…………………………….	Pg. 43
Future Tense – Binyan Pi'el	………………………………..	Pg. 63
Future Tense – Binyan Nif'al	………………………………	Pg. 83
Future Tense – Binyan Pa'al	………………………………..	Pg. 103
Future Tense – Binyan Pa'al 1, Subgroup 1	………………..	Pg. 105
Future Tense – Binyan Pa'al 1, Subgroup 2	………………..	Pg. 123
Future Tense – Binyan Pa'al 1, Subgroup 3	………………..	Pg. 139
Future Tense – Binyan Pa'al 1, Subgroup 4	………………..	Pg. 154
Future Tense – Binyan Pa'al 1, Subgroup 5	………………..	Pg. 167
Future Tense – Binyan Pa'al 1, Subgroup 6	………………..	Pg. 180
Future Tense – Binyan Pa'al 2	……………………………..	Pg. 193
Future Tense – Binyan Pa'al 3	……………………………..	Pg. 210
Prepositions	…………………………………………………	Pg. 237

Copyrighted and owned by Ulpan-Or. Any usage without express permission from Ulpan-Or is prohibited.

כל הזכויות שמורות לאולפן-אור. כל שימוש, העתקה והפצה אסורים.

Introduction

Ulpan-Or *i*Hebrew™ Study Kit Series

This kit is part of *i*Hebrew™ - interactive rapid Hebrew study kit series. It was designed by Orly and Yoel Ganor, the founders of Ulpan-Or, using their revolutionary RLA – *Rapid Language Acquisition* method to help you learn Hebrew quickly and easily.

*i*Hebrew™ study kit series contains text and audio materials, which address Hebrew learning at all levels, starting with the Total Beginner level (Alef) and spanning up to the Very Advanced level (Vav).

This study kit addresses Hebrew verbs with the associated grammar and vocabulary in the Future tense. You will easily learn main verb groups using stories and dialogues in a fun and enjoyable way.

While listening, reading and exercising with this kit you will learn:

* *Five verb groups in the Future tense, including some irregular forms*
* *Verb Imperative form*
* *Use of proper prepositions for building correct sentences*
* *Grammar, necessary for proper Hebrew language structure*

Copyrighted and owned by Ulpan-Or. Any usage without express permission from Ulpan-Or is prohibited.
כל הזכויות שמורות לאולפן-אור. כל שימוש, העתקה והפצה אסורים.

Introduction

Following is a partial list of *i*Hebrew™ series study kits available from Ulpan-Or:

Low and High Beginner Level

1. **Hebrew Alphabet** - addresses print and script letters.
2. **Hebrew Experience** - basic orientation Spoken Hebrew.
3. **Kita Alef** - introductory level study kit.
4. **Verbs, Present Tense** - verbs and grammar for low to high beginner level.

Low and High Intermediate Level

1. **Verbs, Future Tense** - verbs and grammar for intermediate level and up.
2. **Verbs, Past Tense** - verbs and grammar for intermediate level and up.
3. **Dialogues** - dialogues addressing various aspects of life.
4. **Situations & Media** - family / school / work situations and items from the Israeli media.

Low and High Advanced Level

1. **Verbs in a Nutshell** - verbs in all tenses, including irregulars
2. **Advanced Hebrew (Dalet)** - dialogues, stories and media
3. **Very Advanced Hebrew (Hey- Vav)** - dialogues, stories and media

E-Tone® – Online Multimedia Weekly Newspaper issued in three levels:

- **Advanced Beginner - Low intermediate**
- **High Intermediate**
- **Advanced**

We continuously update and improve our existing study materials and continue creating new materials for all levels.

To find out more, please visit our site: **www.ulpanor.com**
Contact us for additional information at: **office@ulpanor.com**

Introduction

Following is a Brief Glance at Ulpan-Or Study Kits

BEGINNER LEVEL

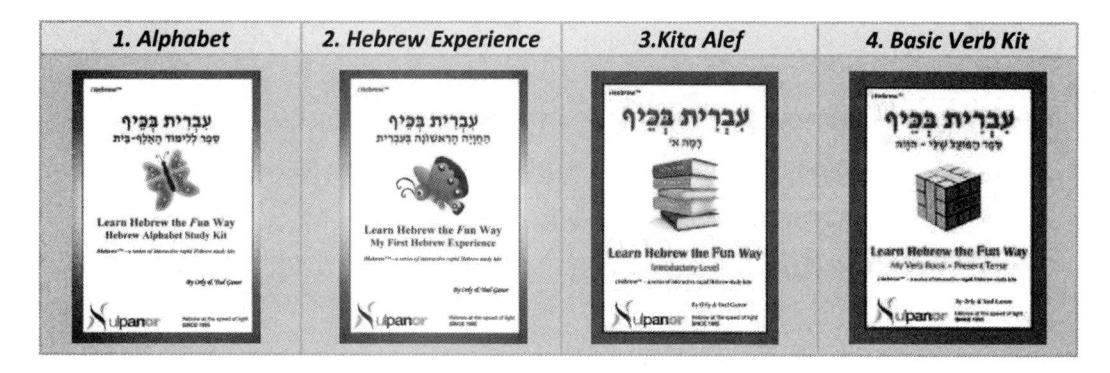

| 1. Alphabet | 2. Hebrew Experience | 3. Kita Alef | 4. Basic Verb Kit |

LOW INTERMEDIATE LEVEL

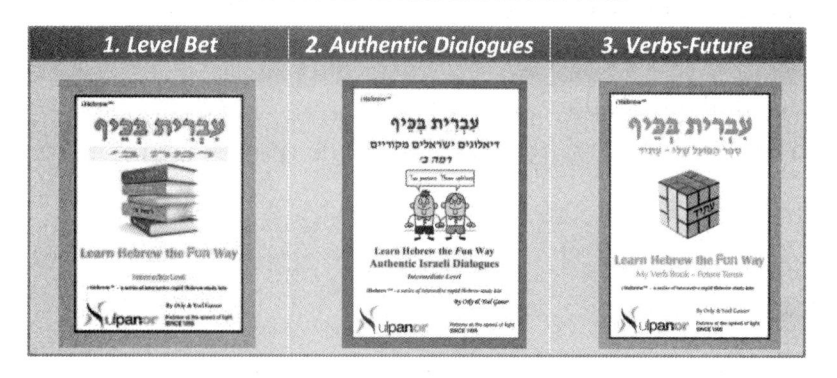

| 1. Level Bet | 2. Authentic Dialogues | 3. Verbs-Future |

HIGH INTERMEDIATE LEVEL

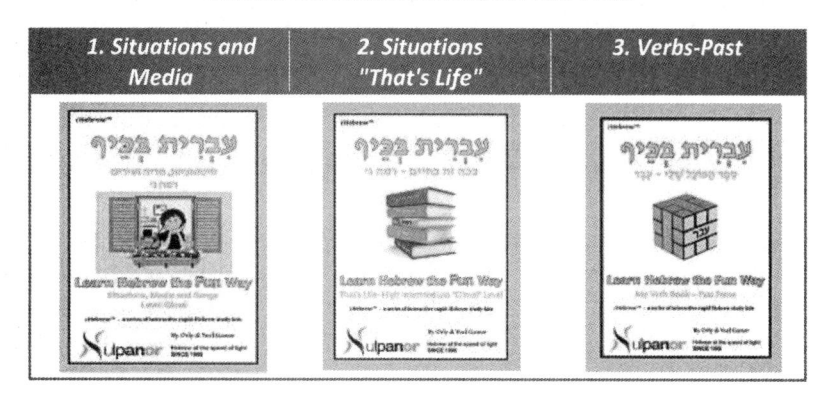

| 1. Situations and Media | 2. Situations "That's Life" | 3. Verbs-Past |

ADVANCED LEVEL

| 1. Verbs in a Nutshell | 2. Advanced Hebrew (Dalet) | 3. Very Advanced Hebrew (Hey - Vav) |

Copyrighted and owned by Ulpan-Or. Any usage without express permission from Ulpan-Or is prohibited.

כל הזכויות שמורות לאולפן-אור. כל שימוש, העתקה והפצה אסורים.

Introduction

Study Instructions

Dear student,

This study kit uses a combined system of recorded and written material. It is of utmost importance to use both – the text and the recorded explanations, to achieve full understanding of the material.

Listen to each track and read the corresponding material 2-3 times and only then move on to new material.

Track 1 contains an affirmation statement. Listen to it, or repeat it by yourself several times a day in order to overcome possible difficulties and barriers in studying Hebrew.

Start studying with the explanation of the general structure of Hebrew verbs on track 2 of CD 1.

Throughout the book there are many types of exercises. It is important that you complete these before moving on to the next section.

After learning each verb tense, please do the exercises. These will let you know how well you are doing, and whether you need to review the material.

Listen to the answers on CDs.

Introduction

Affirmation Statement

I enjoy studying Hebrew. I understand and speak Hebrew easily and fluently. I progress rapidly in Hebrew.

Please repeat this statement when relaxed, as many times a day as possible. Repeating this statement will condition your mind to overcome any barrier in studying Hebrew and will facilitate the studying process tremendously.

Masculine:

אֲנִי נֶהֱנֶה לִלְמוֹד עִבְרִית.
אֲנִי מֵבִין וּמְדַבֵּר עִבְרִית בְּקַלּוּת.
אֲנִי מִתְקַדֵּם מַהֵר בְּעִבְרִית.

Feminine:

אֲנִי נֶהֱנֵית לִלְמוֹד עִבְרִית.
אֲנִי מְבִינָה וּמְדַבֶּרֶת עִבְרִית בְּקַלּוּת.
אֲנִי מִתְקַדֶּמֶת מַהֵר בְּעִבְרִית.

Introduction

Verbs - General Introduction

On the following page you will find the
"HEBREW VERB MENORAH".

As you know, in the Temple there was a golden Menorah built with seven branches. It was made of one single piece of gold to represent the unification of the different…

The Temple Menorah was captured by the Romans after the destruction of the second Temple.

After the foundation of the State of Israel in 1948, the Menorah became the symbol of Israel.

The Hebrew verbs are divided into seven basic groups. Each group is called **"BINYAN"**. (BINYAN = building, structure)

In this book the verb groups are arranged in the shape of a Menorah. (*See next page*).

Important!!

Using this study kit you will learn the Hebrew verbs in a unique and easy way, based **on the sound structure (music, or vowel combination)** that distinguishes the different groups. Once you have learned the music of a certain verb group, you will automatically know how to use all the other verbs having the same music. It will help you be on **"auto-pilot"** and speak like an Israeli.

Let's take a look at the Verb Menorah:

- The 3 branches on the right side represent active verb groups.

- The 3 branches on the left side represent passive verb groups.

- The middle branch represents a group which is sometimes active and sometimes passive.

At this stage please do not plunge into the details. Just absorb the overall picture.

Introduction

מְנוֹרַת הַפֹּעַל
The Verb Menorah

This Menorah represents the fantastic order and music of the Hebrew language. Notice the 3 right-hand branches, which represent active verbs, while the 3 left-hand branches represent passive verbs.
The middle branch represents verbs, which can be both active and passive. *(Listen to CD for explanation and demonstration of the music)*

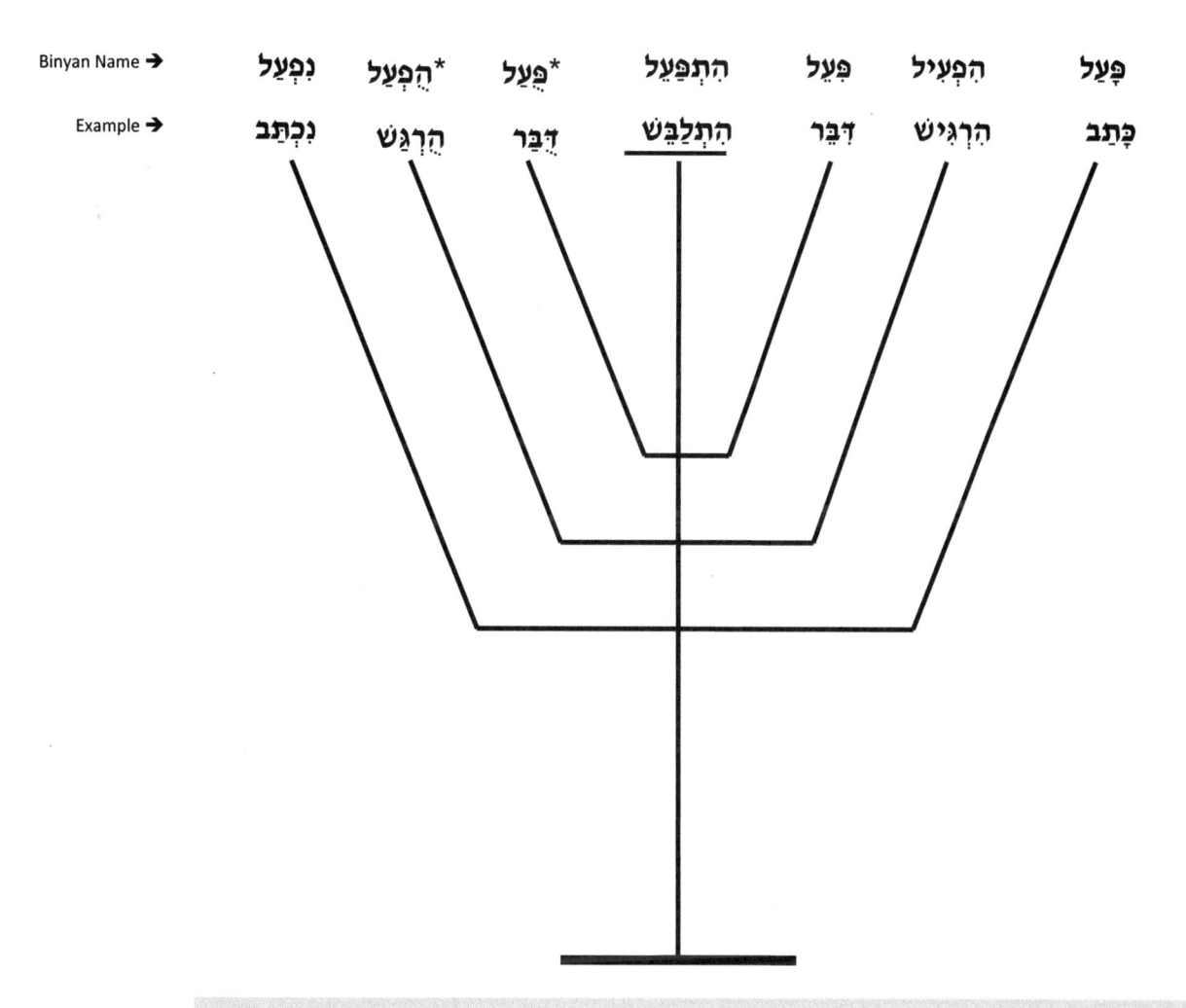

Binyan Name →	נִפְעַל	*הֻפְעַל	*פֻּעַל	הִתְפַּעֵל	פִּעֵל	הִפְעִיל	פָּעַל
Example →	נִכְתַּב	הֻרְגַּשׁ	דֻּבַּר	הִתְלַבֵּשׁ	דִּבֵּר	הִרְגִּישׁ	כָּתַב

The Verb Menorah represents the mystical bond between the Hebrew language and the deeper layers of Judaism and Torah. According to tradition there are certain Psalms that are spiritually beneficial when read as they are written in the shape of Menorah. (For instance Psalm 67).

* The passive verb groups פֻּעַל and הֻפְעַל will be covered in our more advanced book "Verbs in a Nutshell".

Verb Groups – Binyanim

The Hebrew word for verb is פֹּעַל -POAL, which is derived from the root פעל (PA'AL) - **do, act**

Each verb group - **Binyan** (*structure, building*) is called by a name which incorporates the root פעל in the particular and unique way in which it is conjugated and pronounced **in the past tense - third person masculine**.

Each Binyan has its unique music (sound pattern) which is represented by the vowels associated with the letters פ ע ל.

The verbs associated with each Binyan have the same sound pattern as the name of the Binyan and this will be helpful in remembering the verb conjugation.

The first Binyan from the right on the Verb Menorah is named - פָּעַל and it includes verbs such as:

Hebrew	יָשַׁב	שָׁמַע	עָבַד	לָמַד	כָּתַב
Phonetic	YASHAV	SHAMA'	'AVAD	LAMAD	KATAV
English	Sit	hear / listen	work	learn	write

All of these verbs have the vowels **A... A...** in third person in the past tense, which are the same sounds as in the name of Binyan פָּעַל – PA'AL

The rest of the Binyanim are similarly named. They too are distinguished by the vowels (music) in past tense - third person masculine.
Therefore, the verbs representing each Binyan in the Menorah have the same "music" in past tense - third person masculine as the name of each Binyan. (See chart on the next page).

Verb Groups - Binyanim

Examples of the Music (core vowels) of Each Group

Listen to this part on the CD at least twice to get a good feel for the sound pattern.

בִּנְיָן Binyan (name)	Music (vowels)	Example 1	Example 2	Example 3	Remarks
פָּעַל Pa'al	...a...a...	כָּתַב Wrote	לָמַד Studied	יָשַׁב sat	
הִפְעִיל Hif'eel	hi...ee...	הִרְגִּישׁ Felt	הִזְמִין invited	הִפְסִיק stopped	
פִּעֵל Pi'el	...i...e...	דִּבֵּר Spoke	סִפֵּר told	טִיֵּל traveled, toured	
הִתְפַּעֵל Hitpa'el	hit...a...e...	הִתְלַבֵּשׁ got dressed	הִתְחַתֵּן got married	*הִזְדַּקֵן got old	Contains active and passive verbs
פֻּעַל Pu'al	...u...a...	פֻּטַּר was laid off	קֻדַּם was promoted	סֻכַּם was summarized	
הֻפְעַל Huf'al	hu...a...	הֻרְגַּשׁ was felt	הֻזְמַן was invited	הֻפְסַק was stopped	
נִפְעַל Nif'al	ni...a...	נִכְנַס entered	נִלְמַד was learned	נִפְגַּשׁ met (with)	Contains active and passive verbs

*The verb הִזְדַּקֵן sounds a bit different from the pattern, it still belongs to the Hitpa'el Binyan. The explanation is found in the relevant section.

Time Words – Future Tense

Future Tense – General Structure

Before we actually move to the future tense, let's first get familiar with the time words associated with the future in order to be able to make correct sentences.

| Tomorrow | מָחָר |
| Day after tomorrow | מָחֳרָתַיִים |

In Hebrew, in order to say: **next week, next month** and so on, we use the word הַבָּא for masculine or הַבָּאָה for feminine.
It means – "**the coming**".

Example: Next week - בַּשָׁבוּעַ הַבָּא

Pay attention, in Hebrew we have to use the preposition בּ with the noun.

| Month | חֹדֶשׁ |
| Next month | בַּחֹדֶשׁ הַבָּא |

| Year | שָׁנָה |
| Next year | בַּשָׁנָה הַבָּאָה |

When we want to say: **in a week, in a month** and so on, we use the preposition בְּעוֹד.

Example: בְּעוֹד שָׁבוּעַ

| בְּעוֹד... In a... | שָׁבוּעַ |

Copyrighted and owned by Ulpan-Or. Any usage without express permission from Ulpan-Or is prohibited.
כל הזכויות שמורות לאולפן-אור. כל שימוש, העתקה והפצה אסורים.

General Structure of the Future Tense

Future tense in Hebrew is characterized by adding prefixes to the verb "kernel" as opposed to adding suffixes in the past tense. Let's look at the following chart to follow the pattern of the verb structure in future tense.

We divide the chart into two parts:

Pronoun →	אֲנַחְנוּ	הוּא	אַתָּה/הִיא	אֲנִי
Prefix →	נ....	י....	ת....	א....

In the above chart of prefixes we can find connection between the pronouns and the prefixes. Please note that there is a certain correspondence between the first or second letter of the pronoun and the letter of the prefix.

Pronoun →	הֵם / *הֵן	אַתֶּם / *אַתֶּן	אַתְּ
Prefix & Suffix →	י... וּ	ת... וּ	ת... י

In the above chart we can find connection between the pronouns and the prefixes. Please note that there is a certain correspondence between the first or second letter of the pronoun and the letter of the prefix. Here we also find the endings which are always used with the corresponding pronoun.

As we will see the verb "kernel" in the future tense is easily derived from the infinitive form.

* In Modern Hebrew verbs used with feminine pronouns **הן** and **אתן** are usually conjugated in the future tense the same way as for masculine **הם** and **אתם** and therefore the feminine plural form will not be addressed throughout this book.

Future Tense – General Structure

Prefix Patterns - Explanation

Pronoun →	4. אֲנַחְנוּ	3. הוּא	2. אַתָּה/הִיא	1. אֲנִי
Prefix →	נ....	י....	ת....	א....

1. The first letter **א** of **אֲנִי** indicates the **א** of the prefix.
2. The **ת** of **אַתָּה** indicates the **ת** of the prefix.
   The verb pattern for **הִיא** is exactly like for **אַתָּה**.
3. The **ו** of **הוּא** is represented by a **י** as the prefix.
4. The **נ** of **אֲנַחְנוּ** indicates the **נ** of the prefix.

Pronoun →	3. הֵם	2. אַתֶּם	1. אַתְּ
Prefix & Suffix →	י ... וּ	ת ... וּ	ת...י

1. The **ת** of **אַתְּ** indicates the **ת** of the prefix. The ending is always **י**.
2. The **ת** of **אַתֶּם** indicates the **ת** of the prefix. The ending is always **וּ**.
3. The prefix for **הֵם** is **י**, same as for **הוּא**. The ending is always **וּ**.

Future Tense – General Structure

Study and memorize the future pattern charts and fill in the correct prefixes and suffixes for each pronoun in the following tables.

Fill in the following tables without looking at the future pattern charts.

Pronoun →	אֲנַחְנוּ	הוּא	אַתָּה/הִיא	אֲנִי
Prefix →				

Pronoun →	הֵם	אַתֶּם	אַתְּ
Prefix & Suffix →			

Do the same exercise again, if you are still uncertain about the future verb patterns.

Pronoun →	אֲנַחְנוּ	הוּא	אַתָּה/הִיא	אֲנִי
Prefix →				

Pronoun →	הֵם	אַתֶּם	אַתְּ
Prefix & Suffix →			

Future Tense – General Structure

Imperative Form - צִוּוּי

In English for the purpose of expressing verbs in their imperative form, the core verb form is used.

For instance:

To return ⟹ Return!

Example: Return the book!

To write ⟹ Write!

Example: Write me an email, please.

Although there exists a specific imperative structure for the verbs in Hebrew, a lot of times people in Israel just use verbs in their future form for the purpose of expressing imperative condition.

For a negative sentence using the imperative, please note that the equivalent for the English "Don't" is אַל.

לֹא ⟸ אַל

Example:

Go there! – !תֵּלֵךְ לְשָׁם
Don't go there! – !אַל תֵּלֵךְ לְשָׁם

In this study kit we will show examples of the imperative verb form as we learn various respective verb groups.

We will provide an explanation for the specific imperative form structure in our more advanced study kit.

Future Tense – General Structure

Learning the Future Tense – עָתִיד

Phase 1 – absorbing new material

1. Learn structure of the Binyan in future tense

2. Practice conversion to future tense

3. Practice future tense using a story

Phase 2 – internalizing the material

4. Create your own story

5. Take a vocabulary test

6. Practice by creating and answering questions

Copyrighted and owned by Ulpan-Or. Any usage without express permission from Ulpan-Or is prohibited.

כל הזכויות שמורות לאולפן-אור. כל שימוש, העתקה והפצה אסורים.

Binyan Hif'eel

בניין הפעיל

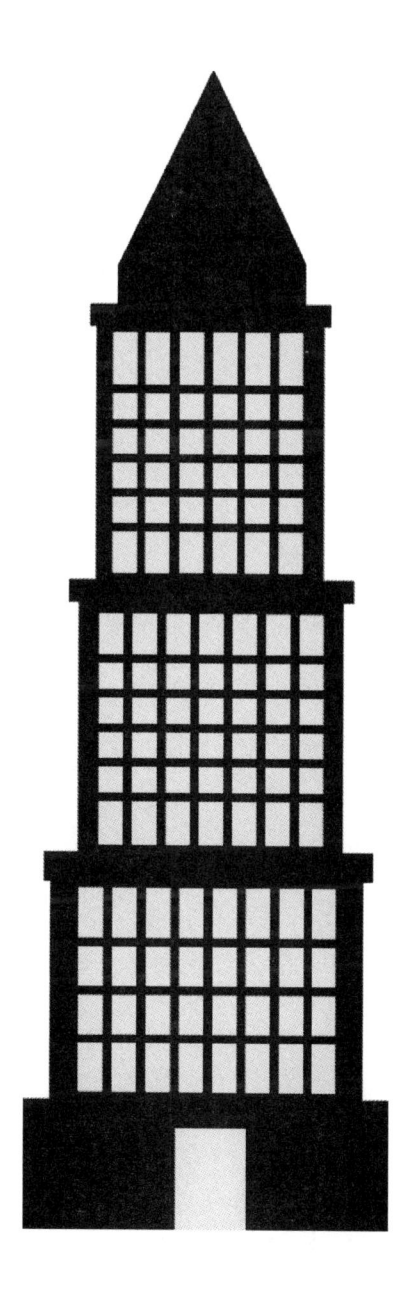

Binyan Hif'eel
בניין הפעיל

Infinitive form of each Binyan is the key to understanding the future tense structure. Let's review it now.

Infinitive Form

The infinitive form of Binyan Hif'eel always begins with לְהַ and the last vowel is י.

So the sound pattern of Binyan Hif'eel is

L'HA...EE...

A...EE... are the core sound pattern vowels

Example:

לְהַרְגִּיש - to feel

Binyan Hif'eel
בניין הפעיל

Moving from Infinitive Form to Future Tense

In Binyan Hif'eel we omit the infinitive form prefix לְהַ, while maintaining the sound pattern of the infinitive form:

...A...EE...

Instead of the לְהַ we use prefixes corresponding to the pronouns.

As an example let's use the verb to feel - לְהַרְגִּיש. Follow the arrows to find the prefixes used for each pronoun.

to feel – לְהַרְגִּיש

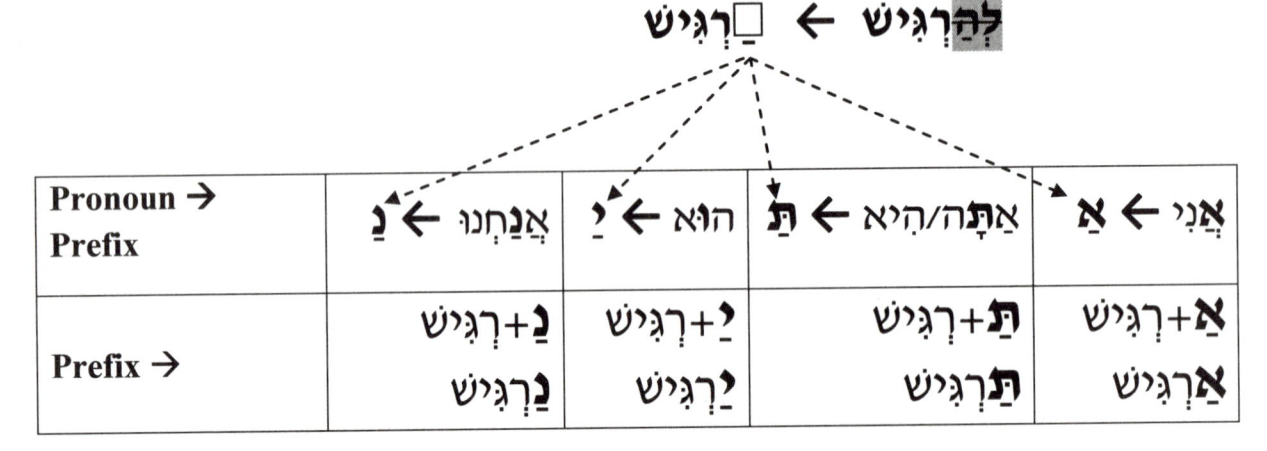

לְהַרְגִּיש ← ☐רְגִּיש

Pronoun → Prefix	אֲנַחְנוּ ← נַ	הוּא ← יַ	אַתָּה/הִיא ← תַּ	אֲנִי ← אַ
Prefix →	נַ+רְגִּיש נַרְגִּיש	יַ+רְגִּיש יַרְגִּיש	תַּ+רְגִּיש תַּרְגִּיש	אַ+רְגִּיש אַרְגִּיש

Now we will also need to add the corresponding suffixes:

Pronoun → Prefix & Suffix	הֵם ← יַ+וּ	אַתֶּם ← תַּ+וּ	אַתְּ ← תַּ+י
Prefix & Suffix →	יַ+רְגִּיש+וּ יַרְגִּישׁוּ	תַּ+רְגִּיש+וּ תַּרְגִּישׁוּ	תַּ+רְגִּיש+י תַּרְגִּישִׁי

1. Learn the structure of the Binyan in future tense

Binyan Hif'eel
בניין הפעיל

Moving from Infinitive Form to Future Tense

Starting with pronouns requiring only a prefix:

שם הפועל באנגלית	שֵׁם פֹּעַל Infinitive	אני	אתה/היא	הוא	אנחנו	את
to feel	לְהַרְגִּישׁ	אַרגיש	תַרגיש	ירגיש	נַרגיש	תרגישי
to begin	לְהַתְחִיל	אַתחיל	תַתחיל	יתחיל	נתחיל	תתחילי
to invite, to order	לְהַזְמִין	אַזמין	תַזמין	יַזמין	נַזמין	תזמיני
to arrive	לְהַגִּיעַ	אַגיע	תַגיע	יגיע	נגיע	תגיעי
to get to know	לְהַכִּיר	אַכּיר	תַכּיר	יכּיר	נכּיר	תכּירי
to understand	לְהָבִין	אָבִין	תָבין	יָבין	נָבין	תָבִיני

Binyan Hif'eel

And now, pronouns which require a suffix as well:

הם	אתם	את	שֵׁם פֹּעַל Infinitive	שם הפועל באנגלית
יַרְגִישׁוּ	תַּרְגִישׁוּ	תַּרְגִישִׁי	לְהַרְגִישׁ	to feel
יתחילו	תתחילו	תתחילי	לְהַתְחִיל	to begin
יזמינו	תזמינו	תזמיני	לְהַזְמִין	to invite, to order
יגיעו	תגיעו	תגיעי	לְהַגִיעַ	to arrive
יכירו	תכירו	תכירי	לְהַכִּיר	to get to know
יבינו	תבינו	תביני	לְהָבִין	to understand

Binyan Hif'eel

CD1 Track 10

Some more verbs, again starting with pronouns requiring only a prefix:

אתם	אנחנו	הוא	אתה/היא	אני	שֵׁם פֹּעַל Infinitive	שם הפועל באנגלית
תאמינו	נַאֲמִין	יַאֲמִין	תַאֲמִין	אַאֲמִין	לְהַאֲמִין	to believe, to trust
תבטיחו	נבטיח	יבטיח	תבטיח	אַבְטִיחַ	לְהַבְטִיחַ	to promise
תחזירו	נחזיר	יחזיר	תחזיר	אַחְזִיר	לְהַחֲזִיר	to return (an object)
תפסיקו	נפסיק	יפסיק	תפסיק	אַפְסִיק	לְהַפְסִיק	to cease
תגידו	נגיד	יגיד	תגיד	אַגִיד	*לְהַגִיד	*to say

*Notice that the verb **להגיד** is **only** used in Hebrew as infinitive and future tense/imperative. It is **never** used in past or present tense

Binyan Hif'eel

And now, pronouns which require a suffix as well:

הם	אתם	את	שֵׁם פֹּעַל Infinitive	שם הפועל באנגלית
יאמינו	תאמינו	תאמיני	לְהַאֲמִין	to believe, to trust
יַבְטִיחוּ	תַבְטִיחוּ	תַבְטִיחִי	לְהַבְטִיחַ	to promise
יַחְזִירוּ	תַחְזִירוּ	תַחְזִירִי	לְהַחֲזִיר	to return (an object)
יַפְסִיקוּ	תַפְסִיקוּ	תַפְסִיקִי	לְהַפְסִיק	to cease
יַגִידוּ	תַגִידוּ	תַגִידִי	*לְהַגִיד	*to say

*Notice that the verb **להגיד** is **only** used in Hebrew as infinitive and future tense/imperative. It is **never** used in past or present tense

Binyan Hif'eel

סִפּוּר: מָה נָכִין לְרֹאשׁ הַשָּׁנָה?

3. Practice future tense using a dialogue

CD1 Track 11

אוֹצַר מִלִּים

to make, to prepare	לְהָכִין
don't	אַל
to get fat	לְהַשְׁמִין
worst comes to worse	מַקְסִימוּם
if you say (so) (f. sg.)	אִם אַתְּ אוֹמֶרֶת
whenever	מָתַי שֶׁ...
comfortable, feel comfortable (f. sg.)	נוֹחַ, תַּרְגִּישִׁי בְּנוֹחַ
to agree	לְהַסְכִּים
who asks him?! (slang)	מִי שׁוֹאֵל אוֹתוֹ?! (סְלֶנְג)

Binyan Hif'eel
סיפור: מה נכין לראש השנה?

דינה: משה, בשבוע הבא ראש השנה. אולי **נזמין** את אילנה חברה שלי?

משה: בבקשה, **תזמיני**, למה לא?

***

דינה: אילנה, מה נשמע? אני רוצה להזמין אותך לראש השנה.

אילנה: בשמחה! אני **אגיע**. מה להכין?

דינה: אל **תכיני** כלום. אנחנו **נכין** הכל.

אילנה: אני לא שואלת אותך. **אכין** עוגה.

דינה: עוגה? לא, אל **תכיני** עוגה... אנחנו **נשמין**.

אילנה: אוי, **תפסיקי**. משה ואת אף פעם לא **תשמינו**. אתם כל כך רזים.

דינה: אנחנו לא רזים בכלל. אבל בסדר, **תכיני** עוגה. מקסימום **נשמין** קצת.

אילנה: **תגידי**, דינה... אני יכולה לשאול אותך משהו, אבל **תרגישי** בנוח לומר לא.

דינה: **ארגיש** בנוח לומר לא. מה את רוצה לשאול?

אילנה: אני יכולה **להביא** (bring) מישהו לארוחה?

דינה: מישהו? מה, יש לך חבר? ואו! אני לא מאמינה!

אילנה: **תאמיני, תאמיני**... יש לי חבר, ואני מאוד רוצה שת**כירו**.

דינה: מצוין, אז **נכיר** בראש השנה. משה, לאילנה יש חבר! היא **תביא** אותו לארוחה!

אילנה: רגע, רגע, דינה! אני לא יודעת אם החבר שלי **יסכים** לבוא.

דינה: מי שואל אותו?! בטח שהוא **יסכים**.

אילנה: טוב, אם את אומרת... באיזו שעה להגיע?

דינה: **תגיעו** מתי שת**גיעו**. לא **נתחיל** לאכול לפני שת**גיעו**.

אילנה: אחלה. אז להתראות בראש השנה, ו... שנה טובה.

Binyan Hif'eel

Now listen and read and check your comprehension sentence by sentence:

Dina: Moshe, Next week is Rosh Hashana. Maybe we'll invite Ilana, my friend (f.)?	דינה: משה, בשבוע הבא ראש השנה. אולי **נזמין** את אילנה חברה שלי?
Moshe: Go ahead, invite (her), why not?	משה: בבקשה, **תזמיני**, למה לא?
Dina: Ilana, how are you? I want to invite you for Rosh Hashana.	דינה: אילנה, מה נשמע? אני רוצה להזמין אותך לראש השנה.
Ilana: Gladly! I'll be there. What should I [to] make?	אילנה: בשמחה! אני **אגיע**. מה להכין?
Dina: Don't make anything. We'll make everything.	דינה: אל **תכיני** כלום. אנחנו **נכין** הכל.
Ilana: I'm not asking you. (I'll) make a cake.	אילנה: אני לא שואלת אותך. **אכין** עוגה.
Dina: A cake? No, don't make a cake… We'll get fat.	דינה: עוגה? לא, אל **תכיני** עוגה... אנחנו **נשמין**.
Ilana: Oh, stop it.	אילנה: אוי, **תפסיקי**.
Moshe and you will never get fat. You're so skinny.	משה ואת אף פעם לא **תשמינו**. אתם כל כך רזים.
Dina: We're not skinny at all. But okay, make a cake.	דינה: אנחנו לא רזים בכלל. אבל בסדר, **תכיני** עוגה.
Worst comes to worse, we'll get fat a little.	מקסימום, **נשמין** קצת.
Ilana: Excellent. Say, Dina… Can I ask you something.	אילנה: מצוין. **תגידי**, דינה... אני יכולה לשאול אותך משהו.
But feel comfortable to say no.	אבל **תרגישי** בנוח לומר לא.
Dina: Okay. (I'll) feel comfortable to say no. What do you want to ask?	דינה: בסדר. **ארגיש** בנוח לומר לא. מה את רוצה לשאול?
Ilana: Can I bring someone to the meal?	אילנה: אני יכולה **להביא** מישהו לארוחה?
Dina: Someone? What, you have a boyfriend? Wow! I don't believe (it)!	דינה: מישהו? מה, יש לך חבר? ואו! אני לא מאמינה!
Ilana: Believe, believe… I have a boyfriend.	אילנה: **תאמיני, תאמיני**... יש לי חבר.

Binyan Hif'eel

And I really want you to get to know (each other).	ואני מאוד רוצה ש**תכירו**.
Dina: Excellent, so we'll get to know (each other) on Rosh Hashana. Moshe, Ilana has a boyfriend!	דינה: מצוין, אז **נכיר** בראש השנה. משה, לאילנה יש חבר!
She'll bring him to the meal!	היא **תביא** אותו לארוחה!
Ilana: Wait, wait, Dina! I don't know if my boyfriend will agree to come.	אילנה: רגע, רגע, דינה! אני לא יודעת אם החבר שלי **יסכים** לבוא.
Dina: Who's asking him?! Of course he'll agree.	דינה: מי שואל אותו?! בטח שהוא **יסכים**.
Ilana: Okay, if you say (so)… At what time should we come [to arrive]?	אילנה: טוב, אם את אומרת... באיזו שעה להגיע?
Dina: (You'll) arrive whenever you arrive.	דינה: **תגיעו** מתי שתגיעו.
We won't start eating before you'll arrive.	לא **נתחיל** לאכול לפני שתגיעו.
Ilana: Cool. So I'll see you on Rosh Hashana, and… Shana Tova.	אילנה: אחלה. אז להתראות בראש השנה, ו... שנה טובה.

Binyan Hif'eel

Check yourself

1. Tell the story in Hebrew while reading the English text.

2. Fill in the right column in Hebrew and check yourself using the text on the previous page.

Dina: Moshe, Next week is Rosh Hashana. Maybe we'll invite Ilana, my friend (f.)?	
Moshe: Go ahead, invite (her), why not?	
Dina: Ilana, how are you? I want to invite you for Rosh Hashana.	
Ilana: Gladly! I'll be there. What should I [to] make?	
Dina: Don't make anything. We'll make everything.	
Ilana: I'm not asking you. (I'll) make a cake.	
Dina: A cake? No, don't make a cake… We'll get fat.	
Ilana: Oh, stop it.	
Moshe and you will never get fat. You're so skinny.	
Dina: We're not skinny at all. But okay, make a cake.	
Worst comes to worse, we'll get fat a little.	
Ilana: Excellent. Say, Dina… Can I ask you something.	
But feel comfortable to say no.	
Dina: Okay. (I'll) feel comfortable to say no. What do you want to ask?	
Ilana: Can I bring someone to the meal?	

Binyan Hif'eel

Dina: Someone? What, you have a boyfriend? Wow! I don't believe (it)!	
Ilana: Believe, believe... I have a boyfriend.	
And I really want you to get to know (each other).	
Dina: Excellent, so we'll get to know (each other) on Rosh Hashana. Moshe, Ilana has a boyfriend!	
She'll bring him to the meal!	
Ilana: Wait, wait, Dina! I don't know if my boyfriend will agree to come.	
Dina: Who's asking him?! Of course he'll agree.	
Ilana: Okay, if you say (so)... At what time should we come [to arrive]?	
Dina: (You'll) arrive whenever you arrive.	
We won't start eating before you'll arrive.	
Ilana: Cool. So I'll see you on Rosh Hashana, and... Shana Tova.	

Binyan Hif'eel

Your Story – Binyan Hif'eel

4. Create your own story

Now create your own story in Hebrew using the above story as an example.

Use all or part of the following verbs in future tense:

get to know; understand; believe/trust; promise; cease; return (an object)

Binyan Hif'eel
בניין הפעיל

Vocabulary Test

Complete the chart according to the example:

הם	את	אתה/היא	אני	שֵׁם פֹּעַל Infinitive	שם הפועל באנגלית
ירגישו	תרגישי	תרגיש	ארגיש	לְהַרְגִּישׁ	to feel
יתחילו	תתחילי	תתחיל	אתחיל	להתחיל	to begin
יזמינו	תזמיני	תזמין	אזמין	להזמין	to invite, to order
יגיעו	תגיעי	תגיע	אגיע	להגיע	to arrive
יכירו	תכירי	תכיר	אכיר	להכיר	to get to know
יבינו	תביני	תבין	אבין	להבין	to understand

Binyan Hif'eel

Vocabulary Test (Cont.)

הם	את	אתה/היא	אני	שֵׁם פֹּעַל Infinitive	שם הפועל באנגלית
יאמינו	תאמיני	תאמין	אאמין	להאמין	to believe, to trust
יבטיחו	תבטיחי	תבטיח	אבטיח	להבטיח	to promise
יחזירו	תחזירי	תחזיר	אחזיר	להחזיר	to return (an object)
יפסיקו	תפסיקי	תפסיק	אפסיק	להפסיק	to cease
יגידו	תגידי	תגיד	אגיד	להגיד	to say

Binyan Hif'eel

Exercising Binyan Hif'eel

6. Practice by creating and answering questions

Listen once to the following questions in order to exercise verbs in this Binyan. Then write the questions in Hebrew. Listen to the audio again and check your translation.

Questions	Hebrew Translation
1. How would you feel after a marathon run?	
2. Will the Messiah arrive next week?	
3. Is it important that all the Jews in the world will know Israel?	
4. Who will always understand you? Who will never understand you?	
5. What will you never believe in?	
6. If we (will) promise you that you'll speak Hebrew like an Israeli, will you believe (it)?	
7. Will we never bring [return] back time?	
8. What will you never stop doing?	

Binyan Hif'eel

Write your answers in Hebrew here:

1.
2.
3.
4.
5.
6.
7.
8.

Binyan Hif'eel

Exercise: Fill in the missing parts in the chart. (You don't have to know the meaning of the verbs). Check yourself by listening to the CD.

Conjugation	Infinitive	Pronoun
	לְהַתְאִים — match	אַתֶּם
	לְהַצְחִיק — make laugh	הוּא
	לְהַסְבִּיר	אֲנַחְנוּ
	לְהַבְלִיג	אַתָּה
	לְהַנְצִיחַ	אַתְּ
	לְהַנְהִיג — to lead	הִיא
	לְהַפְעִיל	הֵם
	לְהַגְשִׁים	אֲנִי

Binyan Hif'eel
Imperative Form of Binyan Hif'eel

Let's use the future tense structure to create imperative form.

Remember: to create negative sentences the equivalent of **"Don't"** is אַל.

Following are some examples of sentences using the imperative form:

Return (m. sg.) the book immediately!	תַּחֲזִיר אֶת הַסֵּפֶר מִיָּד!
Don't order (f. sg.) this food for me!	אַל תַּזְמִינִי אֶת הָאוֹכֶל הַזֶּה בִּשְׁבִילִי!

Exercise: Write your own sentences in English using verbs from Binyan Hif'eel in imperative form. Use both, negative and positive structures.
Translate those to Hebrew in the table below:

English	Hebrew
Do not believe him! (♀)	אל תאמיני אותו!
Stop! (♀)	תפסלי!
Start writing! (♂)	תתחיל לכתוב!
Feel better! (♂♂)	תרגישו יותר טוב!
Save him! (♀)	תצילי אותו!

Binyan Hif'eel

Summary of Binyan Hif'eel

Present and Future Tense

Notice how the basic sound of the Binyan remains the same, as only the suffixes and prefixes alternate.

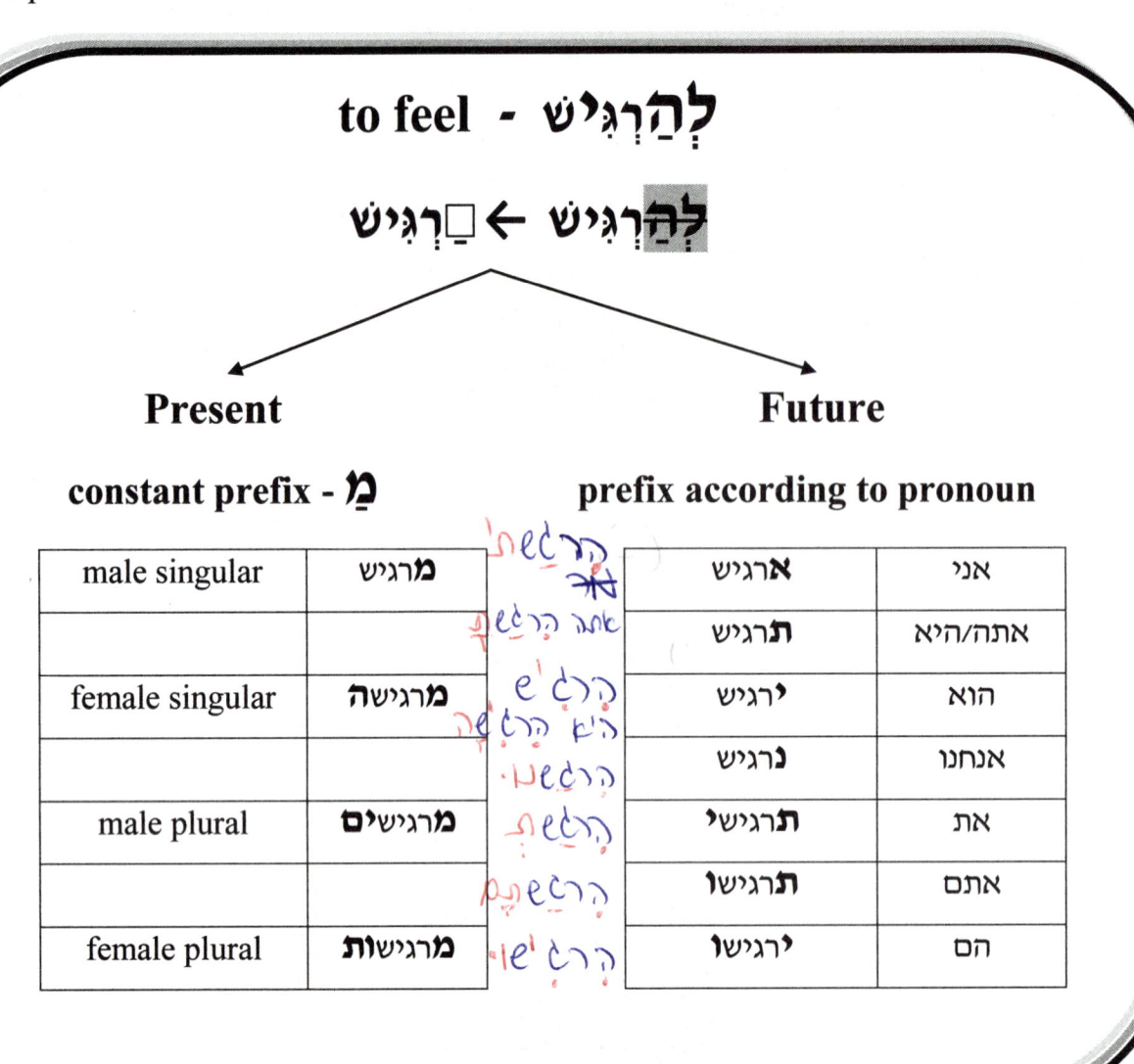

לְהַרְגִּיש - to feel

לְהַרְגִּיש ← ⬜ַרְגִּיש

Present

constant prefix - מַ

male singular	**מ**רגיש	
female singular	**מ**רגישה	
male plural	**מ**רגישים	
female plural	**מ**רגישות	

Future

prefix according to pronoun

ארגיש	אני
תרגיש	אתה/היא
ירגיש	הוא
נרגיש	אנחנו
תרגישי	את
תרגישו	אתם
ירגישו	הם

בניין התפעל

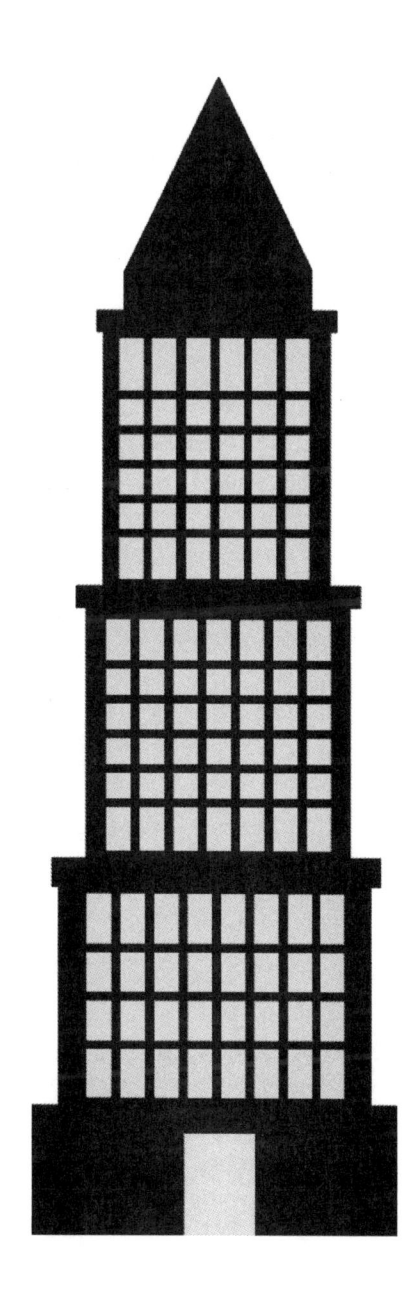

Binyan Hitpa'el

כל הזכויות שמורות לאולפן-אור. כל שימוש, העתקה והפצה אסורים.

Copyrighted and owned by Ulpan-Or. Any usage without express permission from Ulpan-Or is prohibited.
כל הזכויות שמורות לאולפן-אור. כל שימוש, העתקה והפצה אסורים.

CD1 Track 14

Binyan Hitpa'el

Reminder of the infinitve form of the Binyan

בניין התפעל

Infinitive form of each Binyan is the key to understanding the future tense structure. Let's review it now.

Infinitive Form

The infinitive form of Binyan Hitpa'el usually begins with לְהִתְ and the last vowel is **E**. It also has three syllables.

So the sound pattern of Binyan Hitpa'el is

L'hIt...A...E...

I...A...E... are the core sound pattern vowels

Example:

To progress - לְהִתְקַדֵּם

בניין התפעל

Moving from Infinitive Form to Future Tense

In Binyan Hitpa'el we omit the infinitive form prefix לְהִ, while maintaining the sound pattern of the infinitive form:

...IT...A...E...

Instead of the לְהִ we use prefixes corresponding to the pronouns. As an example let's use the verb to progress – לְהִתְקַדֵּם. Follow the arrows to find the prefixes used for each pronoun.

to progress - לְהִתְקַדֵּם

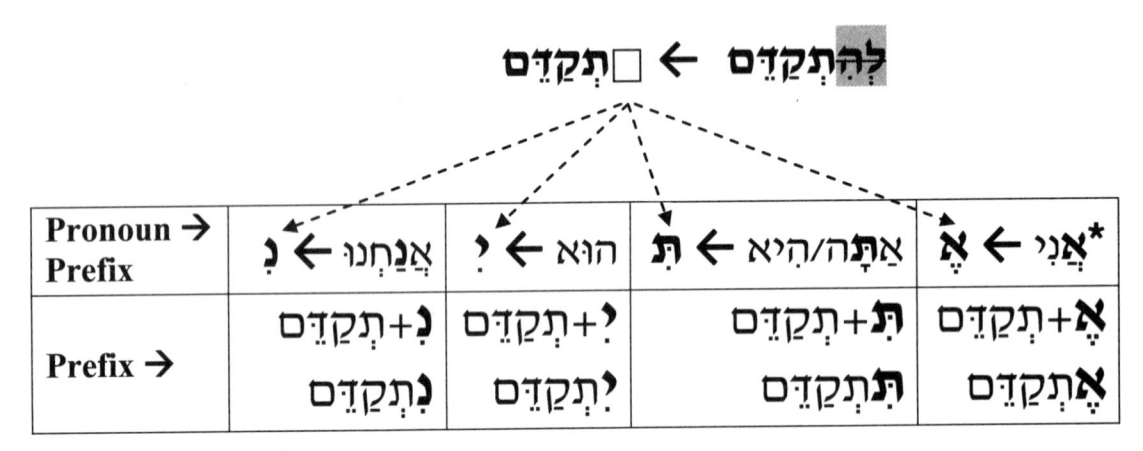

לְהִתְקַדֵּם ← □תְקַדֵּם

Pronoun → Prefix	אֲנַחְנוּ ← נְ	הוּא ← יְ	אַתָּה/הִיא ← תְּ	*אֲנִי ← אֶ
Prefix →	נְ+תְקַדֵּם נִתְקַדֵּם	יְ+תְקַדֵּם יִתְקַדֵּם	תְּ+תְקַדֵּם תִּתְקַדֵּם	אֶ+תְקַדֵּם אֶתְקַדֵּם

Now we will also need to add the corresponding suffixes:

Pronoun → Prefix & Suffix	הֵם ← יְ+וּ	אַתֶּם ← תְּ+וּ	אַתְּ ← תְּ+י
Prefix & Suffix →	יְ+תְקַדְמ+וּ יִתְקַדְמוּ	תְּ+תְקַדְמ+וּ תִּתְקַדְמוּ	תְּ+תְקַדְמ+י תִּתְקַדְמִי

*Note that the music for אֲנִי is "E..A..E..". We will see this phenomenon of אֲנִי being slightly different in other Binyanim as well.

בניין התפעל
Binyan Hitpa'el
Moving from Infinitive Form to Future Tense

Starting with pronouns requiring only a prefix:

אנחנו	הוא	אתה/היא	אני	שֵׁם פֹּעַל Infinitive	שם הפועל באנגלית
נתפלל	יתפלל	תתפלל	אתפלל	לְהִתְפַּלֵּל	to pray
נתלבש	יתלבש	תתלבש	אתלבש	לְהִתְלַבֵּשׁ	to get dressed
נתקדם	יתקדם	תתקדם	אתקדם	לְהִתְקַדֵּם	to progress
נתחתן	יתחתן	תתחתן	אתחתן	לְהִתְחַתֵּן	to get married
נתקשר	יתקשר	תתקשר	אתקשר	לְהִתְקַשֵּׁר	to call, to contact

Binyan Hitpa'el

And now, pronouns which require a suffix as well:

הם	אתם	את	שֵׁם פֹּעַל Infinitive	שם הפועל באנגלית
יִתְפַּלְלוּ	תִתְפַּלְלוּ	תִתְפַּלְלִי	לְהִתְפַּלֵּל	to pray
יתלבשו	תתלבשו	תתלבשי	לְהִתְלַבֵּשׁ	to get dressed
יתקדמו	תתקדמו	תתקדמי	לְהִתְקַדֵּם	to progress
יתחתנו	תתחתנו	תתחתני	לְהִתְחַתֵּן	to get married
יתקשרו	תתקשרו	תתקשרי	לְהִתְקַשֵּׁר	to call, to contact

Binyan Hitpa'el

סִפּוּר: צָרִיךְ לְהִתְחַתֵּן מַהֵר

אוֹצַר מִלִּים

to get rich	לְהִתְעַשֵּׁר
to behave	לְהִתְנַהֵג
to get excited	לְהִתְרַגֵּשׁ
to use	לְהִשְׁתַּמֵּשׁ בְּ...
to get confused	לְהִתְבַּלְבֵּל
to go crazy	לְהִשְׁתַּגֵּעַ
mobile phone	טֶלֶפוֹן סֶלוּלָרִי
no problem! (lit. what's the problem?)	מָה הַבְּעָיָה? אֵין בְּעָיָה?
is saved	שָׁמוּר

3. Practice future tense using a dialogue

Binyan Hitpa'el

סיפור: צריך להתחתן מהר

אבא: מתן, קרן אומרת שאתה עובד בהיי-טק. מה בדיוק אתה עושה בהיי-טק? אתה מנהל?

מתן: מנהל? לא, ממש לא. בעזרת השם, יום אחד **אתקדם** בעבודה שלי, אבל עכשיו אני רק עובד מתחיל.

אבא: אתה צריך להתקדם מהר. אם לא **תתקדם**, לא **תתעשר**! כמה כסף אתה מקבל עכשיו?

קרן: אבא! **תתנהג** יפה!

אבא: איך **אתנהג** יפה? אני רעב, וכשאני רעב אני לא יכול להתנהג יפה. אולי נתחיל לאכול?

אמא: בבקשה, האוכל פה. אפשר להתחיל לאכול. מתן, אתה אוכל טוב? כי קרן ממש לא אוכלת כלום.

מתן: או, אני אוכל יפה מאוד והרבה מאוד.

אמא: מצוין! אם **תתחתנו**, אולי גם קרן תתחיל לאכול.

מתן: באמת? טוב, אז אולי באמת **נתחתן**. קרן, מה את אומרת? **תתחתני** איתי?

אמא ואבא: כן, כן, היא **תתחתן** איתך!

קרן: אמא ואבא, אני צריכה לענות, לא אתם!!! אה... כן, אני חושבת שכן. **אתחתן** איתך.

אמא: או, מזל טוב! קרן, אני הולכת להתקשר לסבא וסבתא. הם כל כך **יתרגשו**!

קרן: רגע, אמא, אל **תתקשרי** לסבא וסבתא. מתן צריך לספר להורים שלו לפני שאת מספרת להורים שלך.

אמא: מה הבעיה? מתן, **תתקשר** להורים שלך עכשיו. נו, **תתקשר**!

מתן: אני לא יכול להתקשר עכשיו. הטלפון הסלולרי שלי בבית.

אמא: מה הבעיה? **תשתמש** בטלפון שלי!

מתן: אני לא זוכר את המספר של ההורים שלי. הוא שמור בזיכרון של הטלפון הסלולרי שלי.

אמא: טוב, אין בעיה. אפשר לנסוע לבית של ההורים שלך. משה, **תתלבש** יפה! אנחנו נוסעים להורים של מתן.

מתן: נוסעים להורים שלי? לא, אני לא יכול לנסוע עכשיו. אני מאוד מתרגש, אני בטוח **אתבלבל** בדרך.

אמא: מתרגש? **תתבלבל** בדרך? או, איזה בחור רומנטי. קרן, **תתפללי** שמתן יהיה רומנטי תמיד. כי אבא שלך... טוב, הוא לא ממש בעל רומנטי.

אבא: סליחה? אני רומנטי מאוד. קרן, **תתפללי** שמתן יהיה בעל טוב כמו אבא שלך.

קרן: אבא, אמא.. די... אני מתחתנת! אפשר בבקשה לשתות יין ולעשות "לחיים"?

אמא: כן, בטח, חמודה. קרן, מתן, לחיים! מתן, **תתנהג** תמיד יפה לבת שלי, כן?

אבא: קרן, מתן, לחיים! מתן, **תתקדם** בעבודה וקרן ואתה **תתעשרו**!

קרן: מתן, לחיים! **תתחתן** איתי מהר, כי עוד רגע אני משתגעת....

Binyan Hitpa'el

Now listen and read and check your comprehension sentence by sentence:

Dad: Matan, Keren says that you work in High-Tech. What exactly do you do in High-Tech? Are you a manager?	אבא : מתן, קרן אומרת שאתה עובד בהיי-טק. מה בדיוק אתה עושה בהיי-טק? אתה מנהל?
Matan: A manager? No, not at all. G-d willing, one day I'll progress at my job, but now I'm only a starting employee.	מתן: מנהל? לא, ממש לא. בעזרת השם, יום אחד **אתקדם** בעבודה שלי, אבל עכשיו אני רק עוֹבֵד מתחיל.
Dad: You need to progress quickly. If you [will not] don't progress, you won't get rich! How much money do you make [get] now?	אבא : אתה צריך להתקדם מהר. אם לא **תתקדם**, לא **תתעשר**! כמה כסף אתה מקבל עכשיו?
Keren: Dad! Behave nicely!	קרן : אבא! **תתנהג** יפה!
Dad: How will I behave nicely? I'm hungry, and when I'm hungry I can't behave nicely. Maybe we'll start eating?	אבא : איך **אתנהג** יפה? אני רעב, וכשאני רעב אני לא יכול להתנהג יפה. אולי נתחיל לאכול?
Mom: Please, the food is here. (We) can start eating. Matan, do you eat well? Because Keren really doesn't eat anything.	אמא : בבקשה, האוכל פה. אפשר להתחיל לאכול. מתן, אתה אוכל טוב? כי קרן ממש לא אוכלת כלום.
Matan: Oh, I eat very nicely and a lot.	מתן : או, אני אוכל יפה מאוד והרבה מאוד.
Mom: Excellent! If you [will] get married, maybe Keren will start to eat too.	אמא : מצוין! אם **תתחתנו**, אולי גם קרן תתחיל לאכול.
Matan: Really? Okay, so maybe we will really get married. Keren, what do you say? Will you marry me?	מתן : באמת? טוב, אז אולי באמת **נתחתן**. קרן, מה את אומרת? **תתחתני** איתי?
Mom and dad: Yes, yes, she'll marry you!	אמא ואבא : כן, כן, היא **תתחתן** איתך!
Keren: Mom and dad – I need to answer, not you! Ah… yes, I think that yes. I'll marry you.	קרן : אמא ואבא- אני צריכה לענות, לא אתם!!! אה... כן, אני חושבת שכן. **אתחתן** איתך.
Mom: Oh, congratulations! Keren, I'm going to call grandpa and grandma. They'll get so excited!	אמא : או, מזל טוב! קרן, אני הולכת להתקשר לסבא וסבתא. הם כל כך **יתרגשו**!
Keren: (Just a) moment, mom, don't call grandpa and grandma. Matan needs to tell his parents before you tell your parents.	קרן : רגע, אמא, אל **תתקשרי** לסבא וסבתא. מתן צריך לספר להורים שלו לפני שאת מספרת להורים שלך.

Copyrighted and owned by Ulpan-Or. Any usage without express permission from Ulpan-Or is prohibited.

כל הזכויות שמורות לאולפן-אור. כל שימוש, העתקה והפצה אסורים.

Binyan Hitpa'el

אמא : מה הבעיה? מתן, **תתקשר** להורים שלך עכשיו. נו, **תתקשר**!	Mom: No problem! Matan, call your parents now. Come on, call!
מתן : אני לא יכול להתקשר עכשיו. הטלפון הסלולרי שלי בבית.	Matan: I can't call now. My mobile phone is at home.
אמא : מה הבעיה? **תשתמש** בטלפון שלי!	Mom: What's the problem? Use my phone!
מתן : אני לא זוכר את המספר של ההורים שלי. הוא שמור בזיכרון של הטלפון הסלולרי שלי.	Matan: I don't remember my parents' number. It's saved on my mobile phone's memory.
אמא : טוב, אין בעיה. אפשר לנסוע לבית של ההורים שלך. משה, **תתלבש** יפה! אנחנו נוסעים להורים של מתן.	Mom: Okay, no problem. (We) can go to your parents' house. Moshe, get dressed nicely! We're going to Matan's parents.
מתן : נוסעים להורים שלי? לא, אני לא יכול לנסוע עכשיו. אני מאוד מתרגש, אני בטוח **אתבלבל** בדרך.	Matan: Going to my parents? No, I can't go now. I'm very excited, I will surely get confused on the way.
אמא : מתרגש? **תתבלבל** בדרך? או, איזה בחור רומנטי.	Mom: Excited? You'll get confused on the way? Oh, what a romantic guy.
קרן, **תתפללי** שמתן יהיה רומנטי תמיד. כי אבא שלך... טוב, הוא לא ממש בעל רומנטי.	Keren, pray that Matan will always be romantic. Because your dad… well, he's not really a romantic husband.
אבא : סליחה? אני רומנטי מאוד. קרן, **תתפללי** שמתן יהיה בעל טוב כמו אבא שלך.	Dad: Excuse me? I'm very romantic. Keren, pray that Matan will be a good husband like your father.
קרן : אבא, אמא.. די... אני מתחתנת! אפשר בבקשה לשתות יין ולעשות "לחיים"?	Keren: Dad, mom… Stop… I'm getting married! Can we please drink wine and have [do] a "Lechayim"?
אמא : כן, בטח, חמודה. קרן, מתן, לחיים! מתן, **תתנהג** תמיד יפה לבת שלי, כן?	Mom: Yes, sure sweetie. Keren, Matan, Lechayim! Matan, you will always behave nicely to my daughter, yes?
אבא : קרן, מתן, לחיים! מתן, **תתקדם** בעבודה וקרן ואתה **תתעשרו**!	Dad: Keren, Matan, Lechayim! Matan, progress at work and Keren and you will get rich!
קרן : מתן, לחיים! **תתחתן** איתי מהר, כי עוד רגע אני משתגעת....	Keren: Matan, Lechayim! Marry me quickly because in one moment I'll go crazy…

Binyan Hitpa'el

Check yourself

1. Tell the story in Hebrew while reading the English text.
2. Fill in the right column in Hebrew and check yourself using the text on the previous page.

Dad: Matan, Keren says that you work in High-Tech. What exactly do you do in High-Tech? Are you a manager?	
Matan: A manager? No, not at all. G-d willing, one day I'll progress at my job, but now I'm only a starting employee.	
Dad: You need to progress quickly. If you [will not] don't progress, you won't get rich! How much money do you make [get] now?	
Keren: Dad! Behave nicely!	
Dad: How will I behave nicely? I'm hungry, and when I'm hungry I can't behave nicely. Maybe we'll start eating?	
Mom: Please, the food is here. (We) can start eating. Matan, do you eat well? Because Keren really doesn't eat anything.	
Matan: Oh, I eat very nicely and a lot.	
Mom: Excellent! If you [will] get married, maybe Keren will start to eat too.	
Matan: Really? Okay, so maybe we will really get married. Keren, what do you say? Will you marry me?	
Mom and dad: Yes, yes, she'll marry you!	
Keren: Mom and dad – I need to answer, not you! Ah… yes, I think that yes. I'll marry you.	
Mom: Oh, congratulations! Keren, I'm going to call grandpa and grandma. They'll get so excited!	

Binyan Hitpa'el

Keren: (Just a) moment, mom, don't call grandpa and grandma. Matan needs to tell his parents before you tell your parents.	
Mom: No problem! Matan, call your parents now. Come on, call!	
Matan: I can't call now. My mobile phone is at home.	
Mom: What's the problem? Use my phone!	
Matan: I don't remember my parents' number. It's saved on my mobile phone's memory.	
Mom: Okay, no problem. (We) can go to your parents' house. Moshe, get dressed nicely! We're going to Matan's parents.	
Matan: Going to my parents? No, I can't go now. I'm very excited, I will surely get confused on the way.	
Mom: Excited? You'll get confused on the way? Oh, what a romantic guy.	
Keren, pray that Matan will always be romantic. Because your dad… well, he's not really a romantic husband.	
Dad: Excuse me? I'm very romantic. Keren, pray that Matan will be a good husband like your father.	
Keren: Dad, mom… Stop… I'm getting married! Can we please drink wine and have [do] a "Lechayim"?	
Mom: Yes, sure sweetie. Keren, Matan, Lechayim! Matan, you will always behave nicely to my daughter, yes?	
Dad: Keren, Matan, Lechayim! Matan, progress at work and Keren and you will get rich!	
Keren: Matan, Lechayim! Marry me quickly because in one moment I'll go crazy…	

Binyan Hitpa'el

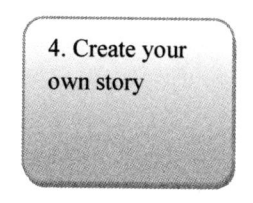

Your Story – Binyan Hitpa'el

Now create your own story in Hebrew using the above story as an example.

Use all or part of the following verbs in future tense:

pray; get dressed; progress; get married; call; contact

[handwritten Hebrew student response]

Binyan Hitpa'el

בניין התפעל

Vocabulary Test

Complete the chart according to the example:

הם	את	אתה/היא	אני	שֵׁם פֹּעַל Infinitive	שם הפועל באנגלית
יתפללו	תתפללי	תתפלל	אתפלל	לְהִתְפַּלֵּל	to pray
				להתלבש	to get dressed
				להתקדם	to progress
				להתחתן	to get married
				להתקשר	to call, to contact

Copyrighted and owned by Ulpan-Or. Any usage without express permission from Ulpan-Or is prohibited.
כל הזכויות שמורות לאולפן-אור. כל שימוש, העתקה והפצה אסורים.

Exercising Binyan Hitpa'el

Binyan Hitpa'el

Listen once to the following questions in order to practice verbs in this Binyan. Then write the questions in Hebrew. Listen to the audio again and check your translation.

Questions	Hebrew Translation
1. Many people in the world will pray for peace. And you?	הרבה אנשים בעולם יתפללו בשלום. ואתה תתפלל?
2. When will you dress up nicely?	מתי אתה תתלבש יפה?
3. In what will you progress this year?	במה אותה תתקדם בשנה הבאה?
4. Will anyone from your family or friends get married soon? Who?	מישהו מהמשפחה אוגדרים שלך יתחתן בקרוב? מי?
5. Who will you call tonight? Why?	מי אתה תתקשר הלילה/למה?
6. What will your family get excited about?	על מה התאסת של משפחה?
7. With whom will you (sg.) debate - לְהִתְוַוכֵּחַ today? About what will you (pl.) debate?	עם מי אתה תתווכח היום? על מה אתם תתווכחו?
8. In a hundred years, do you think people will use a paper and pencil or just a computer?	בעוד מאה שנה אתה חושב שאנשים ישתמשו בנייר ועיפרון או רק במחשב?
9. I will never act like _____, because…	אני אף פעם לא אתנהג כמו ___, כי...

Binyan Hitpa'el

Write your answers in Hebrew here:

1.

2.

3.

4.

5.

6.

7.

8.

9.

Binyan Hitpa'el

Exercise: Fill in the missing parts in the chart. (You don't have to know the meaning of the verbs). Check yourself by listening to the CD.

Conjugation	Infinitive	Pronoun
התגנבתם	להתגנב — to sneak into, to steal into	אַתֶּם
התאפק	להתאפק — restrain oneself	הוּא
התנצלנו	להתנצל — apologize	אֲנַחְנוּ
התכתבת	להתכתב — to correspond c, to exchange letters c	אַתָּה
התמקדת	להתמקד — focus on	אַתְּ
התנשאה	להתנשא — to rise, to be arrogant	הִיא
התגברו	להתגבר — to overcome, to become strong, to intensify	הֵם
התמקצעתי	להתמקצע — to become more professional	אֲנִי

Binyan Hitpa'el

Imperative Form of Binyan Hitpa'el

Let's use the future tense structure to create imperative form.

Remember: to create negative sentences the equivalent of **"Don't"** is **אַל**

Following are some examples of sentences using the imperative form:

Get dressed (f. sg.) quickly !	תִּתְלַבְּשִׁי מַהֵר!
Don't call (m. sg.) me in the morning!	אַל תִּתְקַשֵּׁר אֵלַי בַּבּוֹקֶר!

Exercise: Write your own sentences in English using verbs from Binyan Hitpa'el in imperative form. Use both, negative and positive structures.
Translate those to Hebrew in the table below:

English	Hebrew

Binyan Hitpa'el

Summary of Binyan Hitpa'el
Present and Future Tense

Notice how the basic sound of the Binyan remains the same, as only the suffixes and prefixes alternate.

לְהִתְקַדֵּם - to progress

תְקַדֵּם☐ ← לְהִתְקַדֵּם

Present

constant prefix - מְ

male singular	**מ**תקדם	
female singular	מתקדמ**ת**	
male plural	מתקדמ**ים**	
female plural	מתקדמ**ות**	

Future

prefix according to pronoun

Past tense (handwritten)

אני	**א**תקדם	התקדמתי
אתה/היא	**ת**תקדם	התקשרת
הוא	**י**תקדם	התקשר/ה
אנחנו	**נ**תקדם	התקשרנו
את	**ת**תקדמי	התקשרת
אתם	**ת**תקדמו	התקשרתם
הם	**י**תקדמו	התקשרו

Binyan Pi'el

בניין פיעל

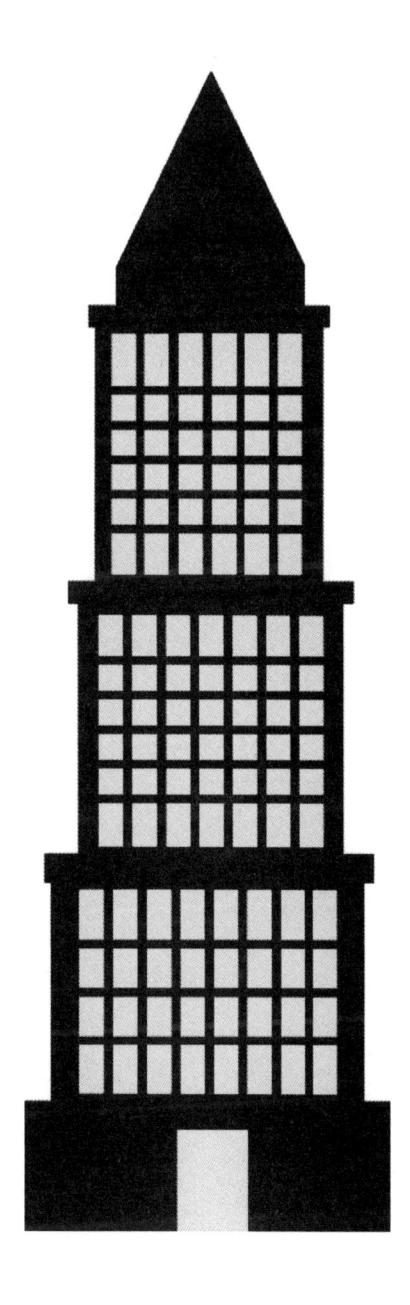

| CD1 Track 20 | Binyan Pi'el | Reminder of the infinitive form of the Binyan |

בניין פיעל

Infinitive form of each Binyan is the key to understanding the future tense structure. Let's review it now.

Infinitive Form

The sound pattern of Binyan Pi'el in the infinitive form is:

lE...A...E...

*(E)...A...E... are the core sound pattern vowels

Example:

to talk – לְדַבֵּר

* The first vowel (E) is in parenthesis because it's part of the prefix sound

Binyan Pi'el

בניין פיעל

Moving from Infinitive Form to Future Tense

1. Learn the structure of the Binyan in future tense

In Binyan Pi'el we omit the infinitive form prefix לְ, while maintaining the sound pattern of the infinitive form:

...(E)...A...E...

Instead of the לְ we use prefixes corresponding to the pronouns.

As an example let's use the verb to talk – לְדַבֵּר. Follow the arrows to find the prefixes used for each pronoun.

לְדַבֵּר – to talk

לְדַבֵּר ← □דַבֵּר

Pronoun → Prefix	נְ ← אֲנַחְנוּ	יְ ← הוּא	תְ ← אַתָּה/הִיא	*אֲ ← אֲנִי
Prefix →	נְ+דַבֵּר נְדַבֵּר	יְ+דַבֵּר יְדַבֵּר	תְ+דַבֵּר תְדַבֵּר	אֲ+דַבֵּר אֲדַבֵּר

Now we will also need to add the corresponding suffixes:

Pronoun → Prefix & Suffix	יְ+וּ ← הֵם	תְ+וּ ← אַתֶּם	תְ+י ← אַתְּ
Prefix & Suffix →	יְ+דַבְּר+וּ יְדַבְּרוּ	תְ+דַבְּר+וּ תְדַבְּרוּ	תְ+דַבְּר+י תְדַבְּרִי

*Note that the music for אֲנִי is "A..A..E.."

Binyan Pi'el

בניין פיעל

Moving from Infinitive Form to Future Tense

Starting with pronouns requiring only a prefix:

שם הפועל באנגלית	שֵׁם פֹּעַל Infinitive	אני	אתה/היא	הוא	אנחנו
to talk	לְדַבֵּר	אֲדַבֵּר	תְּדַבֵּר	יְדַבֵּר	נְדַבֵּר
to tour, to hike	לְטַיֵּיל	אֲטַיֵּיל	תְּטַיֵּיל	יְטַיֵּיל	נְטַיֵּיל
to look for	לְחַפֵּשׂ	אֲחַפֵּשׂ	תְּחַפֵּשׂ	יְחַפֵּשׂ	נְחַפֵּשׂ
to organize, to arrange	לְסַדֵּר	אֲסַדֵּר	תְּסַדֵּר	יְסַדֵּר	נְסַדֵּר
to visit	לְבַקֵּר	אֲבַקֵּר	תְּבַקֵּר	יְבַקֵּר	נְבַקֵּר
to call	לְצַלְצֵל	אֲצַלְצֵל	תְּצַלְצֵל	יְצַלְצֵל	נְצַלְצֵל

Binyan Pi'el
Moving from Infinitive Form to Future Tense (Cont.)

שם הפועל באנגלית	שֵׁם פֹּעַל Infinitive	אני	אתה/היא	הוא	אנחנו
to pay	לְשַׁלֵּם	אֲשַׁלֵּם	תְּשַׁלֵּם	יְשַׁלֵּם	נְשַׁלֵּם
to get, to receive	לְקַבֵּל	אֲקַבֵּל	תְּקַבֵּל	יְקַבֵּל	נְקַבֵּל
to ask, to request	לְבַקֵּשׁ	אֲבַקֵּשׁ	תְּבַקֵּשׁ	יְבַקֵּשׁ	נְבַקֵּשׁ

And now, pronouns which require a suffix as well:

שם הפועל באנגלית	שֵׁם פֹּעַל Infinitive	את	אתם	הם
to talk	לְדַבֵּר	תְּדַבְּרִי	תְּדַבְּרוּ	יְדַבְּרוּ
to tour, to hike	לְטַיֵּל	תְּטַיְּלִי	תְּטַיְּלוּ	יְטַיְּלוּ
to look for	לְחַפֵּשׂ	תְּחַפְּשִׂי	תְּחַפְּשׂוּ	יְחַפְּשׂוּ

Binyan Pi'el
Moving from Infinitive Form to Future Tense (Cont.)

הם	אתם	את	שֵׁם פֹּעַל Infinitive	שם הפועל באנגלית
יְסַדְּרוּ	תְּסַדְּרוּ	תְּסַדְּרִי	לְסַדֵּר	to organize, to arrange
יְבַקְּרוּ	תְּבַקְּרוּ	תְּבַקְּרִי	לְבַקֵּר	to visit
יְצַלְצְלוּ	תְּצַלְצְלוּ	תְּצַלְצְלִי	לְצַלְצֵל	to call
יְשַׁלְּמוּ	תְּשַׁלְּמוּ	תְּשַׁלְּמִי	לְשַׁלֵּם	to pay
יְקַבְּלוּ	תְּקַבְּלוּ	תְּקַבְּלִי	לְקַבֵּל	to get, to receive
יְבַקְּשׁוּ	תְּבַקְּשׁוּ	תְּבַקְּשִׁי	לְבַקֵּשׁ	to ask, to request

Binyan Pi'el

סִפּוּר: דָּג זָהָב

אוֹצַר מִלִּים

fish	דָּג
goldfish	דָּג זָהָב
I wish	הַלְוַואי שֶׁ...
to be late	לְאַחֵר
to cook	לְבַשֵּׁל
what else?	מָה עוֹד?
to play (music)	לְנַגֵּן
financial problems	בְּעָיוֹת פִינַנְסִיוֹת

Binyan Pi'el

סיפור: דג זהב

דג זהב:	שלום, מי את?
הדס:	אני הדס. ואתה?
דג זהב:	אני דג זהב.
הדס:	מה, דג זהב אמיתי?
דג זהב:	כן, דג זהב אמיתי. את יכולה **לבקש** שלושה דברים. מה **תבקשי**?
הדס:	דבר ראשון: **הלוואי שלא אאחר** לעבודה. אני תמיד מאחרת.
דג זהב:	אין בעיה! ממחר בבוקר, לא **תאחרי** לעבודה. תמיד תגיעי בזמן.
הדס:	מצוין, מצוין! דבר שני: הלוואי שבעלי **יבשל** לי ארוחת ערב. הוא לא יודע לבשל, ותמיד אני מבשלת.
דג זהב:	אין בעיה. הערב, בעלך **יבשל** לך ארוחה ואת לא **תבשלי**. מה עוד?
הדס:	עוד דבר אחד, נכון? אממ... אה, אני יודעת! הלוואי שה-Beatles **ינגנו** בישראל!
דג זהב:	אבל ג'ון לנון מת. איך ה-Beatles **ינגנו** בלי ג'ון לנון?
הדס:	אני לא יודעת. אתה דג זהב, אתה יכול לעשות הכל, לא?
דג זהב:	לא כל כך... אני רק דג מתחיל. **תבקשי** משהו אחר, טוב?
הדס:	טוב... הלוואי שבעלי **יסדר** את הבית!
דג זהב:	גם **יבשל** וגם **יסדר**? הדס, אני דג זהב, לא המשיח. **תבקשי** משהו ריאלי, בסדר?
הדס:	בסדר. הלוואי שאמא של בעלי לא **תצלצל** כל שעה.
דג זהב:	לא, לא... אני פוחד מאמא מאמא של בעלך. **תבקשי** משהו אחר.
הדס:	טוב... הלוואי שהחברים שלי ואני **נטייל** בניו-זילנד!
דג זהב:	**טיילו** בניו-זילנד? אבל אין לכם כסף. איך **תשלמו** על הטיול?
הדס:	אני לא יודעת איך **נשלם**. זאת הבעיה שלך, לא שלי. אתה דג זהב, אתה לא יכול לתת לי כסף?
דג זהב:	לא ממש. את מבינה, המנהל שלי בבעיות פיננסיות. **תבקשי** משהו קטן וזול.
הדס:	משהו קטן וזול? ואני באמת **אקבל** את זה?
דג זהב:	כן, **תקבלי**. באמת.
הדס:	בסדר. אני רוצה דג זהב שבאמת יכול לעשות הכל.

Binyan Pi'el

Now listen and read and check your comprehension sentence by sentence:

Goldfish: Hello, who are you?	דג זהב : שלום, מי את?
Hadas: I'm Hadas. And you?	הדס : אני הדס. ואתה?
Goldfish: I'm a goldfish.	דג זהב : אני דג זהב.
Hadas: What, a real goldfish?	הדס : מה, דג זהב אמיתי?
Goldfish: Yes, a real goldfish. You can ask (for) three things. What will you ask (for)?	דג זהב : כן, דג זהב אמיתי. את יכולה לבקש שלושה דברים. מה **תבקשי**?
Hadas: First thing – I wish I won't be late for work. I'm always late.	הדס : דבר ראשון - הלוואי שלא **אאחר** לעבודה. אני תמיד מאחרת.
Goldfish: No problem! As of tomorrow morning, you won't be late for work. You'll always arrive on time.	דג זהב : אין בעיה! ממחר בבוקר, לא **תאחרי** לעבודה. תמיד תגיעי בזמן.
Hadas: Excellent, excellent! Second thing – I wish my husband would cook me dinner. He can't [doesn't know to] cook, and I always cook.	הדס : מצוין, מצוין! דבר שני - הלוואי שבעלי **יבשל** לי ארוחת ערב. הוא לא יודע לבשל, ותמיד אני מבשלת.
Goldfish: No problem. Tonight [this evening], your husband will cook you a meal and you won't cook. What else?	דג זהב : אין בעיה. הערב, בעלך **יבשל** לך ארוחה ואת לא **תבשלי**. מה עוד?
Hadas: One more thing, right? Ahm… oh, I know! I wish that the Beatles will play in Israel!	הדס : עוד דבר אחד, נכון? אממ... אה, אני יודעת! הלוואי שה-Beatles **ינגנו** בישראל!
Goldfish: But John Lennon is dead. How will the Beatles play without John Lennon?	דג זהב : אבל ג'ון לנון מת. איך ה-Beatles **ינגנו** בלי ג'ון לנון?
Hadas: I don't know. You're a goldfish, you can do anything, no?	הדס : אני לא יודעת. אתה דג זהב, אתה יכול לעשות הכל, לא?
Goldfish: Not so much… I'm just a novice fish. Ask for something else, okay?	דג זהב : לא כל כך... אני רק דג מתחיל. **תבקשי** משהו אחר, טוב?
Hadas: Fine… I wish that my husband will organize the house!	הדס : טוב... הלוואי שבעלי **יסדר** את הבית!

Binyan Pi'el

Goldfish: Also cook and also organize? Hadas, I'm a goldfish, not the Messiah.	דג זהב : גם **יבשל** וגם **יסדר**? הדס, אני דג זהב, לא המשיח.
Ask for something realistic, okay?	**תבקשי** משהו ריאלי, בסדר?
Hadas: Okay. I wish that my husband's mom won't call every hour.	הדס : בסדר. הלוואי שאמא של בעלי לא **תצלצל** כל שעה.
Goldfish: No, no… I'm afraid of your husband's mom. Ask for something else.	דג זהב : לא, לא... אני פוחד מאמא של בעלך. **תבקשי** משהו אחר.
Hadas: Okay… I wish that my friends and I will tour in New Zealand.	הדס : טוב... הלוואי שהחברים שלי ואני **נטייל** בניו-זילנד!
Goldfish: Tour in New Zealand? But you don't have money. How will you pay for the trip?	דג זהב : **תטיילו** בניו-זילנד? אבל אין לכם כסף. איך **תשלמו** על הטיול?
Hadas: I don't know how we'll pay (for it). That's your problem, not mine. You're a goldfish, can't you give me money?	הדס : אני לא יודעת איך **נשלם**. זאת הבעיה שלך, לא שלי. אתה דג זהב, אתה לא יכול לתת לי כסף?
Goldfish: Not really. You [understand] see, my manager is in financial problems. Ask for something small and cheap.	דג זהב : לא ממש. את מבינה, המנהל שלי בבעיות פיננסיות. **תבקשי** משהו קטן וזול.
Hadas: Something small and cheap? And I'll really get it?	הדס : משהו קטן וזול? ואני באמת **אקבל** את זה?
Goldfish: Yes, you will get (it). Really.	דג זהב : כן, **תקבלי**. באמת.
Hadas: Okay. I want a goldfish that can really do everything.	הדס : בסדר. אני רוצה דג זהב שבאמת יכול לעשות הכל.

Binyan Pi'el

Check yourself

1. Tell the story in Hebrew while reading the English text.

2. Fill in the right column in Hebrew and check yourself using the text on the previous page.

Goldfish: Hello, who are you?	
Hadas: I'm Hadas. And you?	
Goldfish: I'm a goldfish.	
Hadas: What, a real goldfish?	
Goldfish: Yes, a real goldfish. You can ask (for) three things. What will you ask (for)?	
Hadas: First thing – I wish I won't be late for work. I'm always late.	
Goldfish: No problem! As of tomorrow morning, you won't be late for work. You'll always arrive on time.	
Hadas: Excellent, excellent! Second thing – I wish my husband would cook me dinner. He can't [doesn't know to] cook, and I always cook.	
Goldfish: No problem. Tonight [this evening], your husband will cook you a meal and you won't cook. What else?	
Hadas: One more thing, right? Ahm… oh, I know! I wish that the Beatles will play in Israel!	
Goldfish: But John Lennon is dead. How will the Beatles play without John Lennon?	
Hadas: I don't know. You're a goldfish, you can do anything, no?	
Goldfish: Not so much… I'm just a novice fish. Ask for something else, okay?	

Binyan Pi'el

Hadas: Fine… I wish that my husband will organize the house!	
Goldfish: Also cook and also organize? Hadas, I'm a goldfish, not the Messiah.	
Ask for something realistic, okay?	
Hadas: Okay. I wish that my husband's mom won't call every hour.	
Goldfish: No, no… I'm afraid of your husband's mom. Ask for something else.	
Hadas: Okay… I wish that my friends and I will tour in New Zealand.	
Goldfish: Tour in New Zealand? But you don't have money. How will you pay for the trip?	
Hadas: I don't know how we'll pay (for it). That's your problem, not mine. You're a goldfish, can't you give me money?	
Goldfish: Not really. You [understand] see, my manager is in financial problems. Ask for something small and cheap.	
Hadas: Something small and cheap? And I'll really get it?	
Goldfish: Yes, you will get (it). Really.	
Hadas: Okay. I want a goldfish that can really do everything.	

Binyan Pi'el

Your Story – Binyan Pi'el

4. Create your own story

Now create your own story in Hebrew using the above story as an example.

Use all or part of the following verbs in future tense:

talk; tour/hike; look for; organize/arrange; visit; call; pay; get/receive

Binyan Pi'el

בניין פיעל

Vocabulary Test

5. Take a vocabulary test

Complete the chart according to the example:

הם	את	אתה/היא	אני	שֵׁם פֹּעַל Infinitive	שם הפועל באנגלית
ידברו	תדברי	תדבר	אדבר	לְדַבֵּר	to talk
					to tour, to hike
					to look for
					to organize, to arrange
					to visit
					to call

Copyrighted and owned by Ulpan-Or. Any usage without express permission from Ulpan-Or is prohibited.
כל הזכויות שמורות לאולפן-אור. כל שימוש, העתקה והפצה אסורים.

Binyan Pi'el

Exercising Binyan Pi'el

Listen once to the following questions in order to practice verbs in this Binyan. Then write the questions in Hebrew. Listen to the audio again and check your translation.

Questions	Hebrew Translation
1. What would you cook for a dinner for two?	
2. Who will you visit this week?	
3. Do you think that I'll talk Hebrew better after this course?	
4. Which friends will you call this week?	
5. When will you travel around the world?	
6. Will you fry schnitzels for dinner?	
7. Do you think that you'll tell your children the same stories (סיפורים) that your mother and father told you?	
8. Do you think that Israelis and Palestinians will talk to each other?	
9. Who will you call tonight?	

Binyan Pi'el

Write your answers in Hebrew here:

1.

2.

3.

4.

5.

6.

7.

8.

9.

Binyan Pi'el

Exercise: Fill in the missing parts in the chart. (You don't have to know the meaning of the verbs). Check yourself by listening to the CD.

Conjugation	Infinitive	Pronoun
	לבדר	אַתֶּם
	לנמק	הוּא
	לסמס SMS	אֲנַחְנוּ
	לטפל	אַתָּה
	לצלם	אַתְּ
	לקשקש	הִיא
	לאבד	הֵם
	לסרב	אֲנִי

Binyan Pi'el

Imperative Form of Binyan Pi'el

Let's use the future tense structure to create imperative form.

Remember: to create negative sentences the equivalent of **"Don't"** is אַל.

Following are some examples of sentences using the imperative form:

Don't call (m. sg.) me in the morning!	אַל תְּצַלְצֵל אֵלִי בַּבּוֹקֶר!
Get (f. sg.) your room in order now!	תְּסַדְּרִי אֶת הַחֶדֶר שֶׁלָּךְ עַכְשָׁיו!

Exercise: Write your own sentences in English using verbs from Binyan Pi'el in imperative form. Use both, negative and positive structures.
Translate those to Hebrew in the table below:

English	Hebrew

Binyan Pi'el

Summary of Binyan Pi'el

Present and Future Tense

Notice how the basic sound of the Binyan remains the same, as only the suffixes and prefixes alternate.

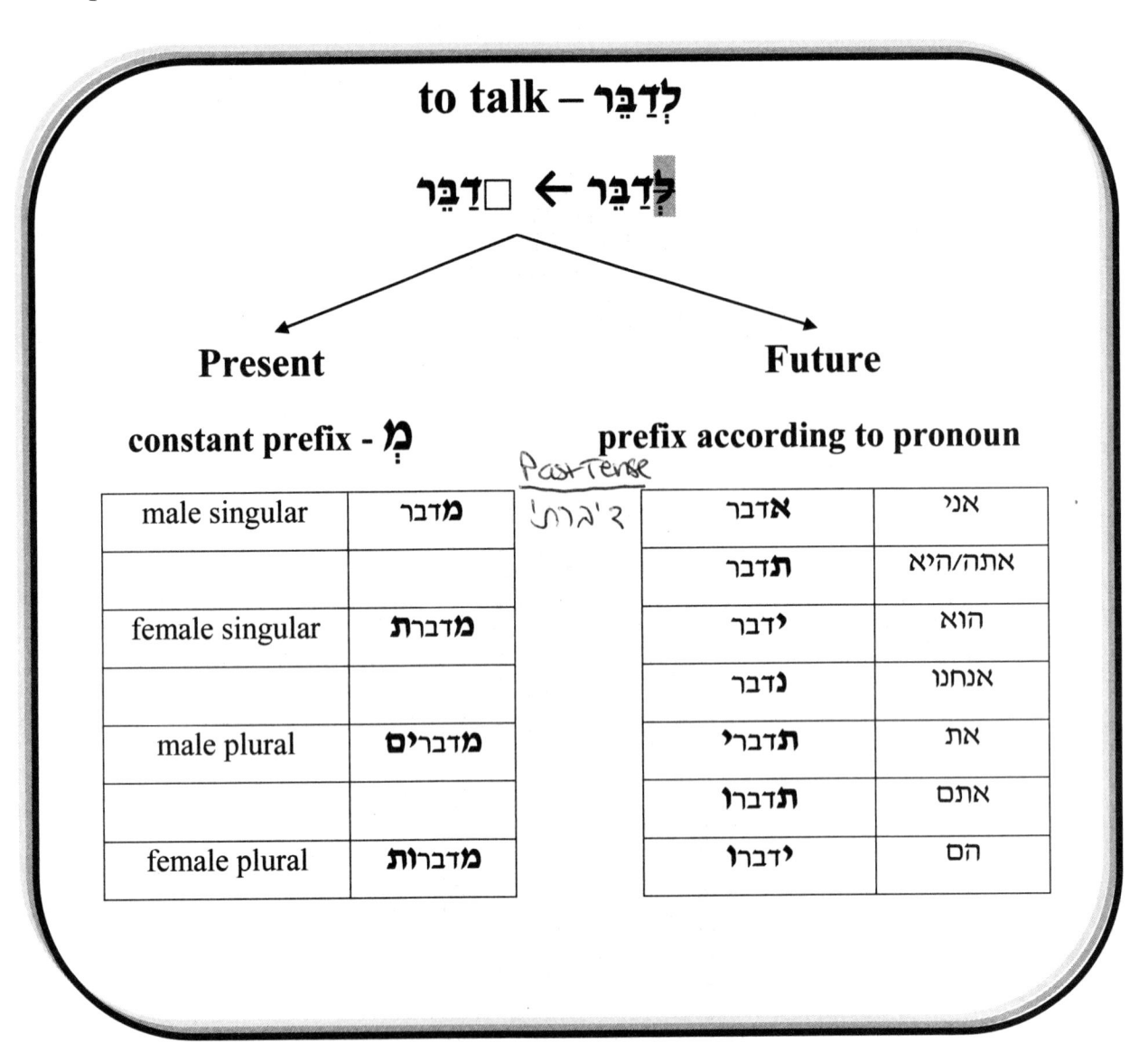

לְדַבֵּר – to talk

לדבר ← ☐דבּר

Present
constant prefix - מְ

male singular	**מדבר**	
female singular	**מדברת**	
male plural	**מדברים**	
female plural	**מדברות**	

Future
prefix according to pronoun

אני	**א**דבר	
אתה/היא	**ת**דבר	
הוא	**י**דבר	
אנחנו	**נ**דבר	
את	**ת**דברי	
אתם	**ת**דברו	
הם	ידברו	

[handwritten note: PAST TENSE / ג׳ורג׳]

Binyan Nif'al

בניין נפעל

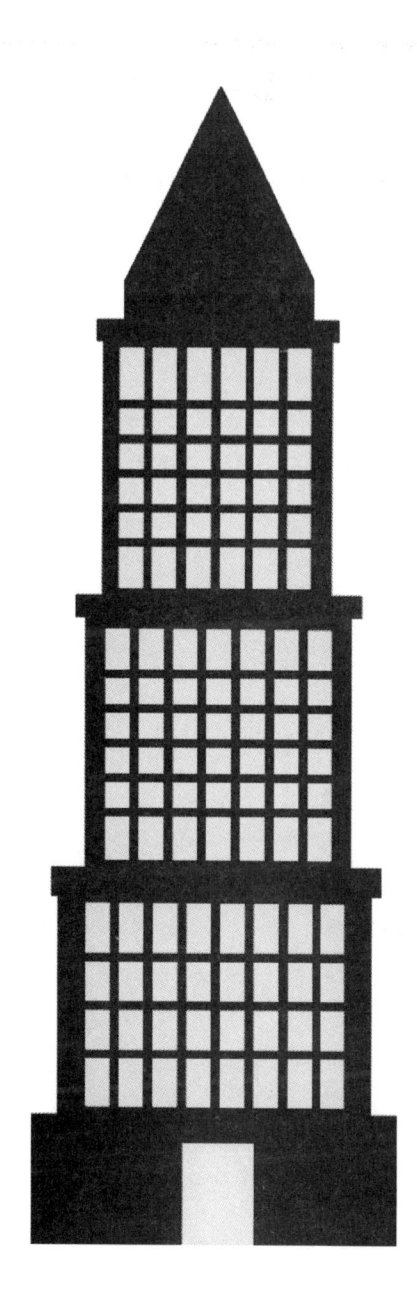

Binyan Nif'al

בניין נפעל

Infinitive form of each Binyan is the key to understanding the future tense structure. Let's review it now.

Infinitive Form

The infinitive form of Binyan Nif'al always begins with לְהִ and the last vowel is **E**. It also has three syllables.

So the sound pattern of Binyan Nif'al is

L'HEE...A...E...

EE...A...E... are the core sound pattern vowels

Example:

To get in - לְהִכָּנֵס

Binyan Nif'al

בניין נפעל

1. Learn the structure of the Binyan in future tense

Moving from Infinitive Form to Future Tense

In Binyan Nif'al we omit the infinitive form prefix לְהִ, while maintaining the sound pattern of the infinitive form:

...EE...A...E...

Instead of the לְהִ we use prefixes corresponding to the pronouns. As an example let's use the verb to get in - לְהִכָּנֵס. Follow the arrows to find the prefixes used for each pronoun.

to get in - לְהִכָּנֵס

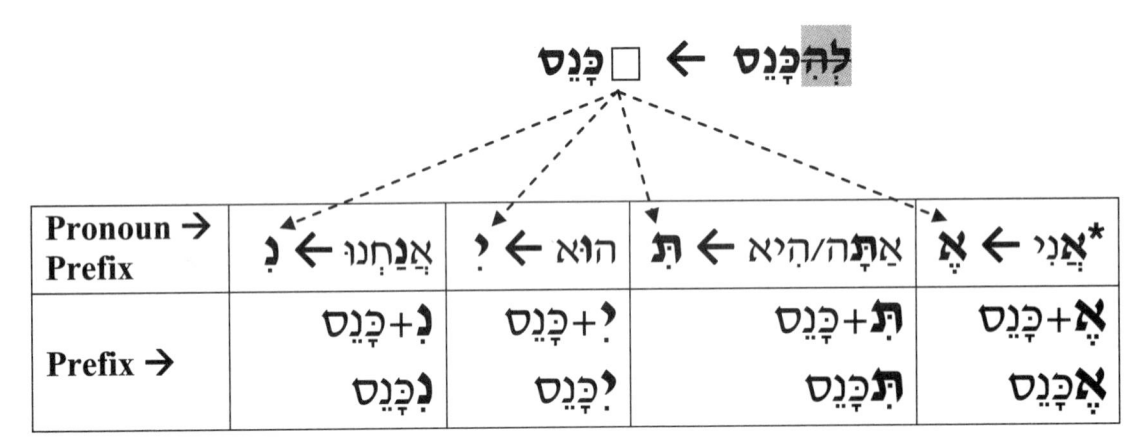

לְהִכָּנֵס ← כָּנֵס □

Pronoun → Prefix	אֲנַחְנוּ ← נְ	הוּא ← יְ	אַתָּה/הִיא ← תְּ	*אֲנִי ← אֶ
Prefix →	נְ+כָּנֵס נִכָּנֵס	יְ+כָּנֵס יִכָּנֵס	תְּ+כָּנֵס תִּכָּנֵס	אֶ+כָּנֵס אֶכָּנֵס

As we add the corresponding suffixes, the 'E' sound disappears:

Pronoun → Prefix & Suffix	הֵם ← יְ+וּ	אַתֶּם ← תְּ+וּ	אַתְּ ← תְּ+י
Prefix & Suffix →	יְ+כָּנֵס+וּ יִכָּנְסוּ	תְּ+כָּנֵס+וּ תִּכָּנְסוּ	תְּ+כָּנֵס+י תִּכָּנְסִי

*Note that the music for אֲנִי is "E..A..E..."

בניין נפעל

Moving from Infinitive Form to Future Tense

Starting with pronouns requiring only a prefix:

אנחנו	הוא	אתה/היא	אני	שֵׁם פֹּעַל Infinitive	שם הפועל באנגלית
נִיכָּנֵס	יִכָּנֵס	תִּיכָּנֵס	אֶכָּנֵס	לְהִכָּנֵס	to enter, to go into
נישאר	ישאר	תישאר	אשאר	לְהִשָּׁאֵר	to stay, to remain
נפגש	יפגש	תפגש	אפגש	לְהִפָּגֵשׁ	to meet (with)
נגמר	יגמר	תגמר	אגמר	לְהִגָּמֵר	to be finished, to end
נבחר	יבחר	תבחר	אבחר	לְהִבָּחֵר	to get elected

Binyan Nif'al

And now, pronouns which require a suffix as well:

הם	אתם	את	שֵׁם פֹּעַל Infinitive	שם הפועל באנגלית
יִיכָּנְסוּ	תִּיכָּנְסוּ	תִּיכָּנְסִי	לְהִיכָּנֵס	to enter, to go into
יִישָׁאֲרוּ	תִּישָׁאֲרוּ	תִּישָׁאֲרִי	לְהִישָׁאֵר	to stay, to remain
יִיפָּגְשׁוּ	תִּיפָּגְשׁוּ	תִּיפָּגְשִׁי	לְהִיפָּגֵשׁ	to meet (with)
יִגָּמְרוּ	תִּגָּמְרוּ	תִּגָּמְרִי	לְהִיגָּמֵר	to be finished, to end
יִבָּחֲרוּ	תִּבָּחֲרוּ	תִּבָּחֲרִי	לְהִיבָּחֵר	to get elected

Binyan Nif'al

סִפּוּר: אוּלַי נֵרָשֵׁם לְיוֹגָה

אוֹצַר מִלִּים

to be opened	לְהִפָּתַח
to register / sign up	לְהֵרָשֵׁם
to fall asleep	לְהֵרָדֵם
to relax	לְהֵרָגַע
to be reminded, to remember	לְהִזָּכֵר
to flip out (slang, lit. to go into movies) don't flip out (f. sg.)	לְהִכָּנֵס לִסְרָטִים אַל תִּכָּנְסִי לִסְרָטִים

Binyan Nif'al

סיפור: אולי נירשם ליוגה

שירלי: דן, בשבוע הבא **ייפתח** קורס יוגה ברחוב שלנו!

דן: יופי! את אוהבת יוגה! אולי **תירשמי** לקורס?

שירלי: כן. אולי **נירשם** יחד?

דן: מי, את ואני? לא, שירלי, אני לא **אירשם** ליוגה.

שירלי: למה לא, דן?

דן: כי זה משעמם. אני **ארדם** אחרי דקה.

שירלי: אני לא חושבת ש**תירדם**, ואני חושבת שיוגה היא דבר מצוין בשבילך.

דן: למה יוגה היא דבר מצוין בשבילי?

שירלי: ביוגה אתה יכול להירגע. כל היום אתה רץ ממקום למקום, עובד קשה... ביוגה, **תירגע** קצת.

דן: אני לא צריך יוגה בשביל להירגע. אני יכול להירגע בבית, מול הטלוויזיה. אולי את **תירגעי** ביוגה, ואני **אשאר** בבית ו**אירגע** מול הטלוויזיה? מה את אומרת?

שירלי: מה אני אומרת? אני אומרת שאני רוצה מאוד ש**נירשם** יחד לקורס, דן. אנחנו אף פעם לא עושים כלום יחד.

דן: זה לא נכון, שירלי, אנחנו עושים הרבה דברים יחד.

שירלי: מה אנחנו עושים יחד? **תיזכר** בדבר אחד, רק דבר אחד! נו, **תיזכר**!

דן: אין בעיה, **אזכר**. מה אנחנו עושים יחד? אה... אנחנו... מממ... טוב, אנחנו לא עושים כלום יחד.

שירלי: אתה רואה?! אנחנו לא עושים כלום יחד! אולי אתה כבר לא אוהב אותי?!

דן: שירלי, באמת, אל **תיכנסי** לסרטים.

שירלי: בסדר, אני לא **אכנס** לסרטים, אבל אני רוצה לדעת למה אתה לא רוצה לעשות איתי כלום.

דן: זה לא זה, שירלי. אני מאוד רוצה לעשות איתך דברים, אבל אני עובד כל היום ו... את יודעת מה, שירלי? אולי **ניפגש** מחר אחרי העבודה במסעדה? **תיפגשי** איתי?

שירלי: איזה כיף! אז **ניפגש** במסעדה, ואחרי זה אולי **נירשם** ליוגה?

דן: שירלי!!!!

שירלי: סתם, סתם. **ניפגש** במסעדה, ואחרי הארוחה אני **אירשם** ליוגה, ואתה **תישאר** בבית עם הטלוויזיה. בסדר?

דן: בסדר גמור.

Binyan Nif'al

Now listen and read and check your comprehension sentence by sentence:

Shirley: Dan, next week a yoga course will be opened on our street!	שירלי: דן, בשבוע הבא **יִיפָּתַח** קורס יוגה ברחוב שלנו!
Dan: Great! You love yoga! Maybe you should [will] register for the course?	דן: יופי! את אוהבת יוגה! אולי **תִּירָשְׁמִי** לקורס?
Shirley: Yes. Maybe we'll register together?	שירלי: כן. אולי **נִירָשֵׁם** יחד?
Dan: Who, you and I? No, Shirley, I won't register for yoga.	דן: מי, את ואני? לא, שירלי, אני לא **אִירָשֵׁם** ליוגה.
Shirley: Why not, Dan?	שירלי: למה לא, דן?
Dan: Because it's boring. I'll fall asleep after (one) minute.	דן: כי זה מְשַׁעֲמֵם. אני **אֵרָדֵם** אחרי דקה.
Shirley: I don't think that you'll fall asleep, and I think that yoga is an excellent thing for you.	שירלי: אני לא חושבת שֶׁ**תֵּירָדֵם**, ואני חושבת שיוגה היא דבר מצוין בשבילך.
Dan: Why is yoga an excellent thing for me?	דן: למה יוגה היא דבר מצוין בשבילי?
Shirley: At yoga you can relax. All day long you run from place to place, work hard… At yoga, you'll relax a bit.	שירלי: ביוגה אתה יכול לְהֵירָגַע. כל היום אתה רץ ממקום למקום, עובד קשה... ביוגה, **תֵּירָגַע** קצת.
Dan: I don't need yoga in order to relax. I can relax at home, in front of the TV. Maybe you'll relax at yoga,	דן: אני לא צריך יוגה בשביל לְהֵירָגַע. אני יכול להירגע בבית, מול הטלוויזיה. אולי את **תֵּירָגְעִי** ביוגה,
and I'll stay at home,	ואני **אֶשָּׁאֵר** בבית,
and relax in front of the TV? What do you say?	וְ**אֵירָגַע** מול הטלוויזיה? מה את אומרת?
Shirley: What do I say? I say that I really want (for us) to register to the course together, Dan. We never do anything together.	שירלי: מה אני אומרת? אני אומרת שאני רוצה מאוד שֶׁ**נִּירָשֵׁם** יחד לקורס, דן. אנחנו אף פעם לא עושים כלום יחד.
Dan: That's not true Shirley, we do a lot of things together.	דן: זה לא נכון, שירלי, אנחנו עושים הרבה דברים יחד.

Binyan Nif'al

Shirley: what do we do together? Remember [be reminded of] one thing, just one thing! Come on, remember!	שירלי: מה אנחנו עושים יחד? **תִּיזָכֵר** בדבר אחד, רק דבר אחד! נו, **תִּיזָכֵר**!
Dan: No problem, I'll remember. What do we do together? Ah… We… Hmm… Okay, we don't do anything together.	דן: אין בעיה, **אֶזָכֵר**. מה אנחנו עושים יחד? אה… אנחנו… מממ… טוב, אנחנו לא עושים כלום יחד.
Shirley: You see?! We don't do anything together! Maybe you don't love me anymore?	שירלי: אתה רואה?! אנחנו לא עושים כלום יחד! אולי אתה כבר לא אוהב אותי?
Dan: Shirley, really, don't flip out.	דן: שירלי, באמת, אל **תִּיכָּנְסִי** לסרטים.
Shirley: Okay, I won't flip out, but I want to know why you don't want to do anything with me.	שירלי: בסדר, אני לא **אֶכָּנֵס** לסרטים, אבל אני רוצה לדעת למה אתה לא רוצה לעשות איתי כלום.
Dan: That's not it, Shirley. I really want to do things with you, but I work all day long and… You know what, Shirley? Maybe we'll meet tomorrow after work at a restaurant? Will you meet [with] me?	דן: זה לא זה, שירלי. אני מאוד רוצה לעשות איתך דברים, אבל אני עובד כל היום ו… את יודעת מה, שירלי? אולי **נִיפָּגֵשׁ** מחר אחרי העבודה במסעדה? **תִּיפָּגְשִׁי** איתי?
Shirley: How fun! So we'll meet at a restaurant, and after that maybe we'll register for yoga?	שירלי: איזה כיף! אז **נִיפָּגֵשׁ** במסעדה, ואחרי זה אולי **נִירָשֵׁם** ליוגה?
Dan: Shirley!	דן: שירלי!!!!
Shirley: Just kidding. We'll meet at the restaurant,	שירלי: סתם, סתם. **נִיפָּגֵשׁ** במסעדה,
and after the meal I'll register for yoga, and you'll stay at home with the TV. Okay?	ואחרי הארוחה אני **אִירָשֵׁם** ליוגה, ואתה **תִּישָּׁאֵר** בבית עם הטלוויזיה. בסדר?
Dan: Definitely okay.	דן: בסדר גמור.

Binyan Nif'al

Check yourself

1. Tell the story in Hebrew while reading the English text.

2. Fill in the right column in Hebrew and check yourself using the text on the previous page

Shirley: Dan, next week a yoga course will be opened on our street!	
Dan: Great! You love yoga! Maybe you should [will] register for the course?	
Shirley: Yes. Maybe we'll register together?	
Dan: Who, you and I? No, Shirley, I won't register for yoga.	
Shirley: Why not, Dan?	
Dan: Because it's boring. I'll fall asleep after (one) minute.	
Shirley: I don't think that you'll fall asleep, and I think that yoga is an excellent thing for you.	
Dan: Why is yoga an excellent thing for me?	
Shirley: At yoga you can relax. All day long you run from place to place, work hard... At yoga, you'll relax a bit.	
Dan: I don't need yoga in order to relax. I can relax at home, in front of the TV. Maybe you'll relax at yoga,	
and I'll stay at home,	
and relax in front of the TV? What do you say?	
Shirley: What do I say? I say that I really want (for us) to register to the course together, Dan. We never do anything together.	

Binyan Nif'al

Dan: That's not true Shirley, we do a lot of things together.	
Shirley: what do we do together? Remember [be reminded of] one thing, just one thing! Come on, remember!	
Dan: No problem, I'll remember. What do we do together? Ah… We… Hmm… Okay, we don't do anything together.	
Shirley: You see?! We don't do anything together! Maybe you don't love me anymore?	
Dan: Shirley, really, don't flip out.	
Shirley: Okay, I won't flip out, but I want to know why you don't want to do anything with me.	
Dan: That's not it, Shirley. I really want to do things with you, but I work all day long and… You know what, Shirley? Maybe we'll meet tomorrow after work at a restaurant? Will you meet [with] me?	
Shirley: How fun! So we'll meet at a restaurant, and after that maybe we'll register for yoga?	
Dan: Shirley!	
Shirley: Just kidding. We'll meet at the restaurant,	
and after the meal I'll register for yoga, and you'll stay at home with the TV. Okay?	
Dan: Definitely okay.	

Binyan Nif'al

4. Create your own story

Your Story – Binyan Nif'al

Now create your own story in Hebrew using the above story as an example.

Use all or part of the following verbs in future tense:

enter; stay; meet; be finished; get elected

Binyan Nif'al

בניין נפעל

Vocabulary Test

5. Take a vocabulary test

Complete the chart according to the example:

הם	את	אתה/היא	אני	שֵׁם פֹּעַל Infinitive	שם הפועל באנגלית
ייכנסו	תיכנסי	תיכנס	אכנס	לְהִכָּנֵס	to enter, to go into Enter
					to stay, to remain STAY
					to meet (with)
					to be finished, to end
					to get elected

Binyan Nif'al

6. Practice by creating and answering questions

Exercising Binyan Nif'al

Listen once to the following questions in order to exercise verbs in this Binyan. Then write the questions in Hebrew. Listen to the audio again and check your translation.

Questions	Hebrew Translation
1. When will you (f.) enter your office tomorrow?	
2. Do you think that the prime minister will get elected again?	
3. How long will you stay in Israel?	
4. Will your friends meet with you this week?	

Binyan Nif'al

Write your answers in Hebrew here:

.1

.2

.3

.4

Binyan Nif'al

Exercise: Fill in the missing parts in the chart. (You don't have to know the meaning of the verbs). Check yourself by listening to the CD.

Conjugation	Infinitive	Pronoun
תצמדו	להיצמד	אַתֶּם
יעלם	להיעלם	הוּא
נדבר	להידבר	אֲנַחְנוּ
תילחם (fight)	להילחם	אַתָּה
תבדל	להיבָּדל (separate)	אַתְּ
תחשב	להיחשב	הִיא
יכנעו	להיכנע (to surrender)	הֵם
אימדד	להימדד	אֲנִי

Binyan Nif'al

Imperative Form of Binyan Nif'al

Let's use the future tense structure to create imperative form.

Remember: to create negative sentences the equivalent of **"Don't"** is אַל.

Following are some examples of sentences using the imperative form:

Get (pl. m.) into the house!	תִּכָּנְסוּ הַבַּיְתָה!
Don't stay (m. sg.) here!	אַל תִּישָׁאֵר כָּאן!

Exercise: Write your own sentences in English using verbs from Binyan Nif'al in imperative form. Use both, negative and positive structures.
Translate those to Hebrew in the table below:

English	Hebrew

Binyan Nif'al

Summary of Binyan Nif'al
Present and Future Tense

Notice how the basic sound of the Binyan remains the same, as only the suffixes and prefixes alternate.

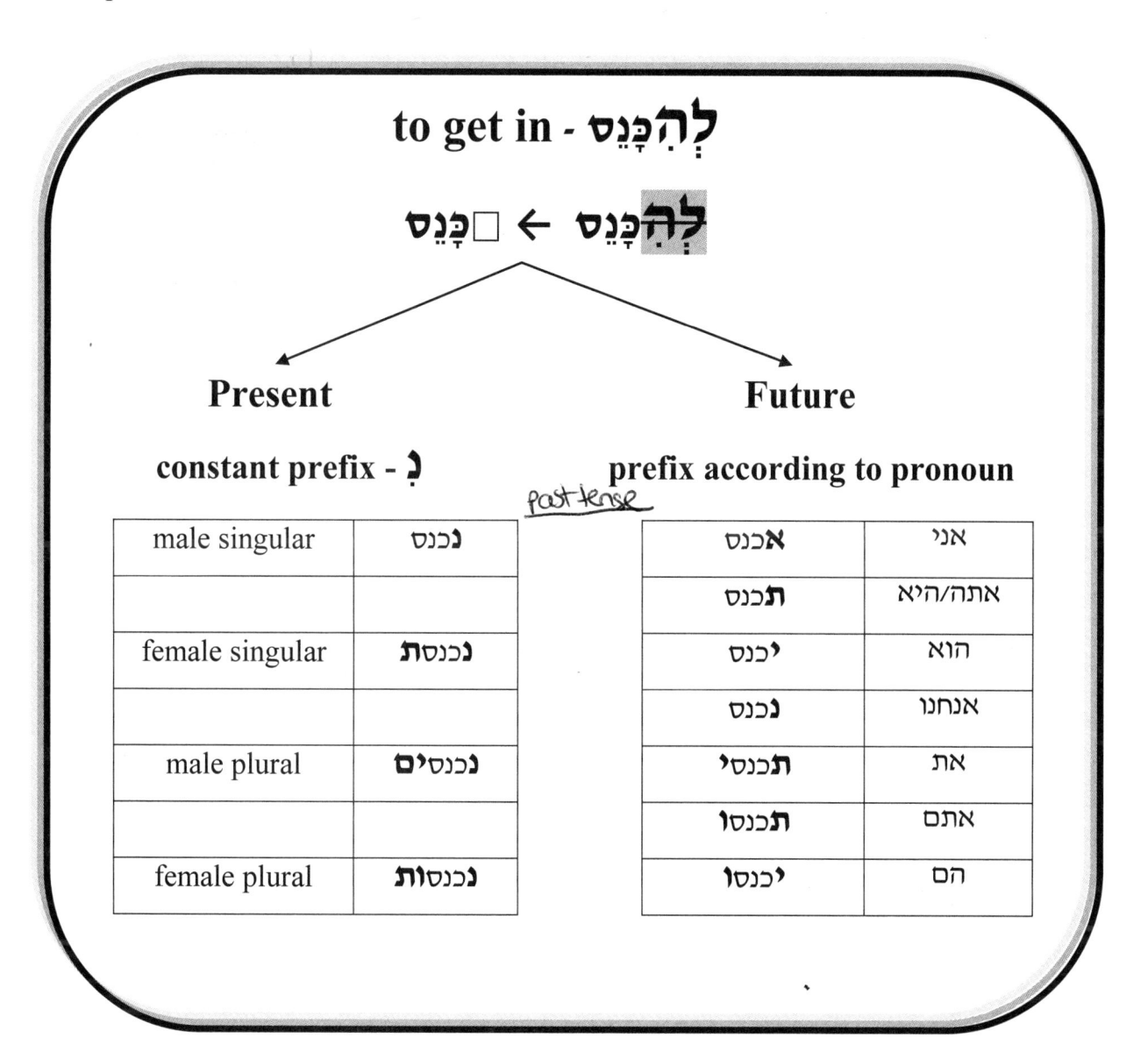

to get in - לְהִכָּנֵס

לְהִכָּנֵס ← □כָּנֵס

Present
constant prefix - נִ

male singular	נכנס
female singular	נכנסת
male plural	נכנסים
female plural	נכנסות

Future
prefix according to pronoun

past tense

אני	אכנס
אתה/היא	תכנס
הוא	יכנס
אנחנו	נכנס
את	תכנסי
אתם	תכנסו
הם	יכנסו

בניין פעל

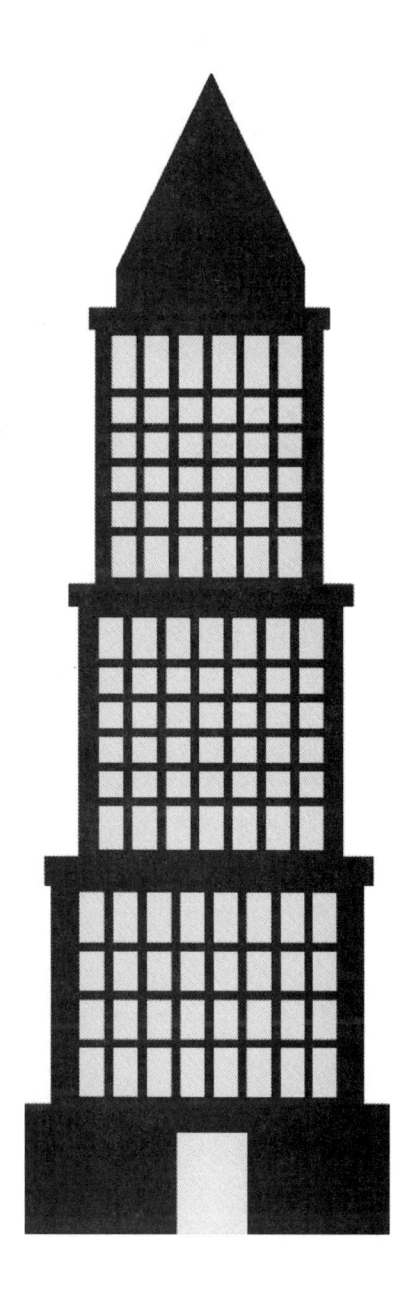

Binyan Pa'al

| CD2 Track 7 | Binyan Pa'al, Group 1, Subgroup 1 | Reminder of the infinitive form of the Binyan |

בניין פעל 1, תת-קבוצה 1

Infinitive form of each Binyan is the key to understanding the future tense structure. Let's review it now.

Infinitive Form

The infinitive form of subgroup 1 has the sound pattern:

LEE...O...

*(EE)...O... are the core sound pattern vowels

Example:

לִכְתּוֹב - to write

* The first vowel (EE) is in parenthesis because it's part of the prefix sound

Binyan Pa'al, Group 1, Subgroup 1

בניין פעל 1, תת-קבוצה 1

Moving from Infinitive Form to Future Tense

In this group we omit the infinitive form prefix לְ, while maintaining the sound pattern of the infinitive form:

...EE...O...

Instead of the לְ we use prefixes corresponding to the pronouns. As an example let's use the verb to write – לִכְתּוֹב. Follow the arrows to find the prefixes used for each pronoun.

to write - לִכְתּוֹב

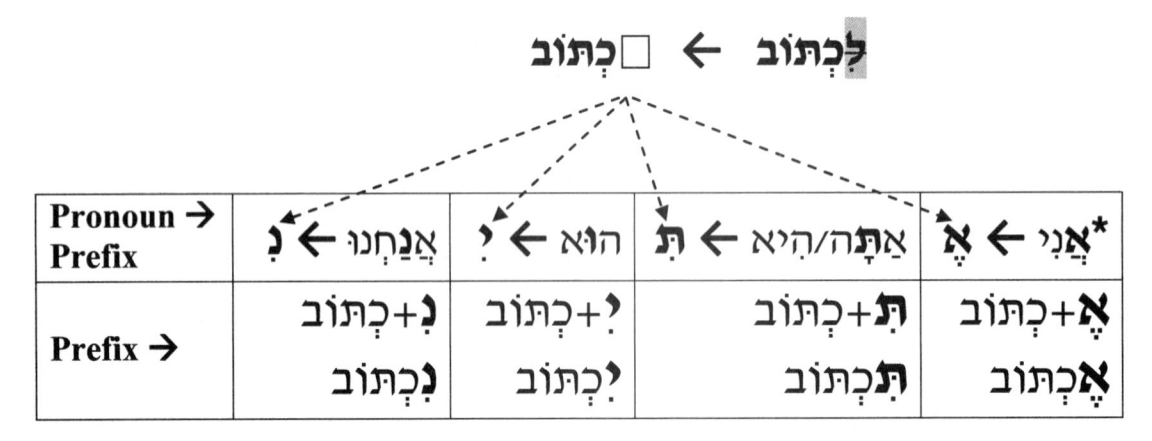

לִכְתּוֹב ← ☐כְתּוֹב

Pronoun → Prefix	אֲנַחְנוּ ← נ	הוּא ← י	אַתָּה/הִיא ← תּ	*אֲנִי ← אֶ
Prefix →	נ+כְתּוֹב נִכְתּוֹב	י+כְתּוֹב יִכְתּוֹב	תּ+כְתּוֹב תִּכְתּוֹב	אֶ+כְתּוֹב אֶכְתּוֹב

As we add the corresponding suffixes, the 'O' sound disappears:

Pronoun → Prefix & Suffix →	הֵם ← י+ו	אַתֶּם ← תּ+ו	אַתְּ ← תּ+י
Prefix & Suffix →	י+כְתְב+ו יִכְתְּבוּ	תּ+כְתְב+ו תִּכְתְּבוּ	תּ+כְתְב+י תִּכְתְּבִי

*Note that the music for אֲנִי is "E...O..."

בניין פעל 1, תת-קבוצה 1

Moving from Infinitive Form to Future Tense

Starting with pronouns requiring only a prefix:

אנחנו	הוא	אתה/היא	אני	שֵׁם פֹּעַל Infinitive	שם הפועל באנגלית
נכתוב	יכתוב	תכתוב	אֶכתוב	לִכְתֹּב	to write
נפגוש	יפגוש	תפגוש	אפגוש	לִפְגֹּש	to meet
נזכור	יזכור	תזכור	אזכור	לִזְכֹּר	to remember
נגמור	יגמור	תגמור	אגמור	לִגְמֹר	to finish

Binyan Pa'al, Group 1, Subgroup 1

And now, pronouns which require a suffix as well:

הם	אתם	את	שֵׁם פֹּעַל Infinitive	שם הפועל באנגלית
יִכְתְּבוּ	תִּכְתְּבוּ	תִּכְתְּבִי	לִכְתֹּב	to write
יִפְגְּשׁוּ	תִּפְגְּשׁוּ	תִּפְגְּשִׁי	לִפְגֹּשׁ	to meet
יִזְכְּרוּ	תִּזְכְּרוּ	תִּזְכְּרִי	לִזְכֹּר	to remember
יִגְמְרוּ	תִּגְמְרוּ	תִּגְמְרִי	לִגְמֹר	to finish

Binyan Pa'al, Group 1, Subgroup 1

Group 1, Supgroup 1 – Irregulars

Many popular and useful verbs belong to Binyan Pa'al, Group 1, Subgroup 1

Some of them have a slightly different sound pattern in the future tense.

The difference of the irregular verbs in this group is in the ending of:
אֲנִי, אַתָּה, הִיא, הוּא, אֲנַחְנוּ

The ending here has the sound "**A**" as opposed to the sound "**O**" of the regular verbs in this group.

For example, regular verbs have the pattern **E… O…** or **EE…O**
"**E**CHT**O**V" אֲנִי אֶכְתֹּב

Irregular verbs in this group have the pattern **E…A…**
"**E**LB**A**SH" אֲנִי אֶלְבַּשׁ

There are three sub-groups of irregular verbs that have the **E…A…** sound pattern.

Group A The last root letter is a guttural letter: ע, א, ח	Group B The middle root letter is a guttural letter: ע, א, ח	Group C Here we show three popular verbs with the E…A… pattern:
לִשְׁמֹעַ	לִצְחֹק (to laugh)	לִלְמֹד
לִפְתֹּחַ	לִצְעֹק (to shout)	לִלְבֹּשׁ
לִקְרֹא	לִדְאֹג (to worry)	לִשְׁכַּב

		לִצְעֹק	לִדְאֹג	לִצְחֹק	לִקְרֹא	לִשְׁמֹעַ	לִפְתֹּחַ	לִלְבֹּשׁ	לִשְׁכַּב	לִלְמֹד	
אֲנִי	אֶלְמַד										
אַתָּה	תִּלְמַד										
הוּא	יִלְמַד										
אֲנַחְנוּ	נִלְמַד										
אַתְּ	תִּלְמְדִי										
אַתֶּם	תִּלְמְדוּ										
הֵם	יִלְמְדוּ										

Binyan Pa'al, Group 1, Subgroup 1

שְׁאֵלוֹת

לִלְמֹד - אֵיפֹה **תִּלְמַד** עִבְרִית?

מָתַי **תִּלְמַד** לְדַבֵּר עִבְרִית טוֹבָה?

לִשְׁכַּב - **תִּשְׁכְּבוּ** לִישֹׁן בַּבֹּקֶר?

מָתַי הַחֲבֵרִים שֶׁלָּךְ **יִשְׁכְּבוּ** לִישֹׁן?

לִלְבֹּשׁ - מַה **תִּלְבְּשִׁי** לַמְּסִבָּה?

Verbs with guttural root letters (א, ע, ח)

לִפְתֹּחַ - _ _ ח - מָתַי יִפְתְּחוּ אֶת הַבַּנְק מָחָר?

לִשְׁמֹעַ - _ _ ע - תִּשְׁמַע חֲדָשׁוֹת בְּעִבְרִית הָעֶרֶב?

לִקְרֹא - _ _ א - אֵיפֹה תִּקְרְאִי סֵפֶר טוֹב?

לִצְחֹק - _ ח _ - עִם מִי תִּצְחֲקִי?

לִצְעֹק - _ ע _ - מָתַי הַיִּשְׂרָאֵלִים יִצְעֲקוּ?

לִדְאֹג - _ א _ - תִּדְאֲגִי לַמִּשְׁפָּחָה שֶׁלָּךְ בְּאָמֶרִיקָה?

Translate the following sentences to Hebrew.

Don't = אַל

Don't shout.	אַל תִּצְעַק.
Don't worry.	
Don't laugh at me.	
When will you lie down tonight?	
How will you remember new words?	
Which book will you read this week?	

Binyan Pa'al, Group 1, Subgroup 1

סִפּוּר: אֵיךְ אֶזְכּוֹר אֶת הַפְּגִישָׁה?

אוֹצַר מִלִּים

בע״מ = בְּעֵרָבוֹן מוּגְבָּל	Ltd.
בְּסֵדֶר גָּמוּר	very well
הָרֶגַע הָאַחֲרוֹן	the last moment
יוֹמָן	calendar

סיפור: איך אזכור את הפגישה?

משה: שלום, זו המזכירה של אריה?

מזכירה: כן, זו המזכירה של אריה.

משה: שלום. מדבר משה, המנהל של "משה ורפי בע"מ". רפי ואני רוצים לפגוש את אריה היום. **נפגוש** אותו ב- 2:00, בקפה "הלל" בירושלים.

מזכירה: בסדר גמור. אריה?

אריה: כן?

מזכירה: משה ורפי **יפגשו** אותך היום, ב- 2:00, בקפה "הלל" בירושלים.

אריה: היום?!?! אוי, הישראלים האלה, תמיד ברגע האחרון! לא, אני לא יכול לפגוש אותם היום. **אפגוש** אותם מחר.

מזכירה: בסדר גמור. משה?

משה: כן?

מזכירה: אריה לא יכול לפגוש אתכם היום. הוא **יפגוש** אתכם מחר.

משה: מחר? לא, מחר לא טוב. מחר רפי ואני **נגמור** לעבוד רק ב- 10:00 בלילה.

מזכירה: ממממ.. אני מבינה. אריה?

אריה: כן?

מזכירה: משה ורפי **יגמרו** לעבוד רק ב- 10:00 בלילה מחר.

אריה: אני מבין. טוב, **אפגוש** אותם בשבוע הבא.

מזכירה: בסדר. משה?

משה: כן?

מזכירה: אריה **יפגוש** אתכם בשבוע הבא, בסדר?

משה: בשבוע הבא? זה עוד הרבה זמן. איך **אזכור** את הפגישה?

מזכירה: אולי **תכתוב** ביומן?

משה: אין לי יומן.

מזכירה: אולי תגיד לאשתך שיש לך פגישה? אשתך בטח **תזכור**. נשים זוכרות הכל.

משה: כן... טוב, אגיד לאשתי, היא באמת **תזכור**. בסדר גמור. **נפגוש** את אריה ביום שני הבא, בקפה "הלל" בירושלים. להתראות!

מזכירה: להתראות!

Binyan Pa'al, Group 1, Subgroup 1

Now listen and read and check your comprehension sentence by sentence:

Moshe: Hello, is this Arieh's secretary?	משה: שלום, זו הַמַזְכִּירָה של אריה? *(mascara)*
Secretary: Yes, this is Arieh's secretary.	מזכירה: כן, זו המזכירה של אריה.
Moshe: Hello. This is [speaking] Moshe, the manager of "Moshe and Rafi Ltd". Rafi and I want to meet Arieh today. We'll meet him at 2:00 in café "Hilel" in Jerusalem.	משה: שלום. מדבר משה, המנהל של "משה ורפי בע"מ". רפי ואני רוצים לפגוש את אריה היום. **נפגוש** אותו ב-2:00, בקפה "הלל" בירושלים.
Secretary: Very well. Arieh?	מזכירה: בסדר גמור. אריה?
Arieh: Yes?	אריה: כן?
Secretary: Moshe and Rafi will meet you today at 2:00, in café "Hilel" in Jerusalem.	מזכירה: משה ורפי **יפגשו** אותך היום, ב-2:00, בקפה "הלל" בירושלים.
Arieh: Today?! Oh, these Israelis, always at the last moment! No, I can't meet them today. I'll meet them tomorrow.	אריה: היום?! אוי, הישראלים האלה, תמיד ברגע האחרון! לא, אני לא יכול לפגוש אותם היום. **אפגוש** אותם מחר.
Secretary: Very well. Moshe?	מזכירה: בסדר גמור. משה?
Moshe: Yes?	משה: כן?
Secretary: Arieh can't meet you today. He'll meet you tomorrow.	מזכירה: אריה לא יכול לפגוש אתכם היום. הוא **יפגוש** אתכם מחר.
Moshe: Tomorrow? No, tomorrow is not good. Tomorrow Rafi and I will only finish working at 10 PM at night.	משה: מחר? לא, מחר לא טוב. מחר רפי ואני **נגמור** לעבוד רק ב-10:00 בלילה.
Secretary: Hmm... I understand. Arieh?	מזכירה: מממ.. אני מבינה. אריה?
Arieh: Yes?	אריה: כן?
Secretary: Moshe and Rafi will only finish working at 10 PM at night tomorrow.	מזכירה: משה ורפי **יגמרו** לעבוד רק ב-10:00 בלילה מחר.
Arieh: I understand. Okay, I'll meet them next week.	אריה: אני מבין. טוב, **אפגוש** אותם בשבוע הבא.

Binyan Pa'al, Group 1, Subgroup 1

Secretary: Okay. Moshe?	מזכירה: בסדר. משה?
Moshe: Yes?	משה: כן?
Secretary: Arieh will meet you next week, okay?	מזכירה: אריה **יפגוש** אתכם בשבוע הבא, בסדר?
Moshe: Next week? That's in a long time. How will I remember the meeting?	משה: בשבוע הבא? זה עוד הרבה זמן. איך **אזכור** את הפגישה?
Secretary: Maybe you should [will] write (it) in your calendar?	מזכירה: אולי **תכתוב** ביומן?
Moshe: I don't have a calendar.	משה: אין לי יומן.
Secretary: Maybe you should tell your wife that you have a meeting? Your wife will surely remember. Women remember everything.	מזכירה: אולי תגיד לאשתך שיש לך פגישה? אשתך בטח **תזכור**. נשים זוכרות הכל.
Moshe: Yes… well, I'll tell my wife, she'll really remember.	משה: כן... טוב, אגיד לאשתי, היא באמת **תזכור**.
Very well. We'll meet Arieh next Monday, at café "Hilel" in Jerusalem. See you later!	בסדר גמור. **נפגוש** את אריה ביום שני הבא, בקפה "הלל" בירושלים. להתראות!
Secretary: See you later!	מזכירה: להתראות!

Binyan Pa'al, Group 1, Subgroup 1

Check yourself

1. Tell the dialogue in Hebrew while reading the English text.

2. Fill in the right column in Hebrew and check yourself using the text on the previous page.

Moshe: Hello, is this Arieh's secretary?	
Secretary: Yes, this is Arieh's secretary.	
Moshe: Hello. This is [speaking] Moshe, the manager of "Moshe and Rafi Ltd". Rafi and I want to meet Arieh today. We'll meet him at 2:00 in café "Hilel" in Jerusalem.	
Secretary: Very well. Arieh?	
Arieh: Yes?	
Secretary: Moshe and Rafi will meet you today at 2:00, in café "Hilel" in Jerusalem.	
Arieh: Today?! Oh, these Israelis, always at the last moment! No, I can't meet them today. I'll meet them tomorrow.	
Secretary: Very well. Moshe?	
Moshe: Yes?	
Secretary: Arieh can't meet you today. He'll meet you tomorrow.	
Moshe: Tomorrow? No, tomorrow is not good. Tomorrow Rafi and I will only finish working at 10 PM at night.	
Secretary: Hmm… I understand. Arieh?	
Arieh: Yes?	
Secretary: Moshe and Rafi will only finish working at 10 PM at night tomorrow.	

Binyan Pa'al, Group 1, Subgroup 1

Arieh: I understand. Okay, I'll meet them next week.	
Secretary: Okay. Moshe?	
Moshe: Yes?	
Secretary: Arieh will meet you next week, okay?	
Moshe: Next week? That's in a long time. How will I remember the meeting?	
Secretary: Maybe you should [will] write (it) in your calendar?	
Moshe: I don't have a calendar.	
Secretary: Maybe you should tell your wife that you have a meeting? Your wife will surely remember. Women remember everything.	
Moshe: Yes… well, I'll tell my wife, she'll really remember.	
Very well. We'll meet Arieh next Monday, at café "Hilel" in Jerusalem. See you later!	
Secretary: See you later!	

Binyan Pa'al, Group 1, Subgroup 1

4. Create your own story

Your Story – Binyan Pa'al 1, Subgroup 1

Now create your own story in Hebrew using the above story as an example.

Use all or part of the following verbs in future tense:

write; meet; remember; finish

Binyan Pa'al, Group 1, Subgroup 1

בניין פעל 1, תת-קבוצה 1

Vocabulary Test

5. Take a vocabulary test

Complete the chart according to the example:

הם	את	אתה/היא	אני	שֵׁם פֹּעַל Infinitive	שם הפועל באנגלית
יכתבו	**תכתבי**	**תכתוב**	אכתוב	**לִכְתֹּב**	to write
					to meet
					to remember
					to finish

Binyan Pa'al, Group 1, Subgroup 1

6. Practice by creating and answering questions

Exercising Binyan Pa'al 1, Subgroup 1

Listen once to the following questions in order to practice verbs in this group. Then write the questions in Hebrew. Listen to the audio again and check your translation.

Questions	Hebrew Translation
1. What will you always remember? What will you never remember?	
2. If you [will] meet King David, what would you say to him?	
3. Who will write you an email today?	
4. When will we finish all of our wars?	

Write your answers in Hebrew here:

1.

2.

3.

4.

Binyan Pa'al, Group 1, Subgroup 1

Exercise: Fill in the missing parts in the chart. (You don't have to know the meaning of the verbs). Check yourself by listening to the CD.

Conjugation	Infinitive	Pronoun
תנצרו	לנצור	אַתֶּם
יצבוט	לצבוט	הוּא
נזלוג	לזלוג	אֲנַחְנוּ
תקרוב	לצרוב	אַתָּה
תקטפי	לקטוף pick (food)	אַתְּ
תדרוש	לדרוש	הִיא
ישובו	לנשוב	הֵם
אגלוש	לגלוש	אֲנִי

Binyan Pa'al, Group 1, Subgroup 1

Imperative Form of Binyan Pa'al 1, Subgroup 1

Let's use the future tense structure to create imperative form.

Remember: to create negative sentences the equivalent of **"Don't"** is **אַל**

Following are some examples of sentences using the imperative form:

Don't write (f. sg.) me an e-mail.	אַל תִּכְתְּבִי לִי אִימֵייל.
Call me.	תְּצַלְצְלִי אֵלִי.
Meet (m. sg.) me in the restaurant in the evening.	תִּפְגּוֹשׁ אוֹתִי בַּמִסְעָדָה בָּעֶרֶב.

Exercise: Write your own sentences in English using verbs from Binyan Pa'al 1, Subgroup 1 in imperative form. Use both, negative and positive structures. Translate those to Hebrew in the table below:

English	Hebrew

Binyan Pa'al, Group 1, Subgroup 1

Summary of Binyan Pa'al 1, Subgroup 1
Present and Future Tense

Notice how the basic sound of the Binyan remains the same, as only the suffixes and prefixes alternate.

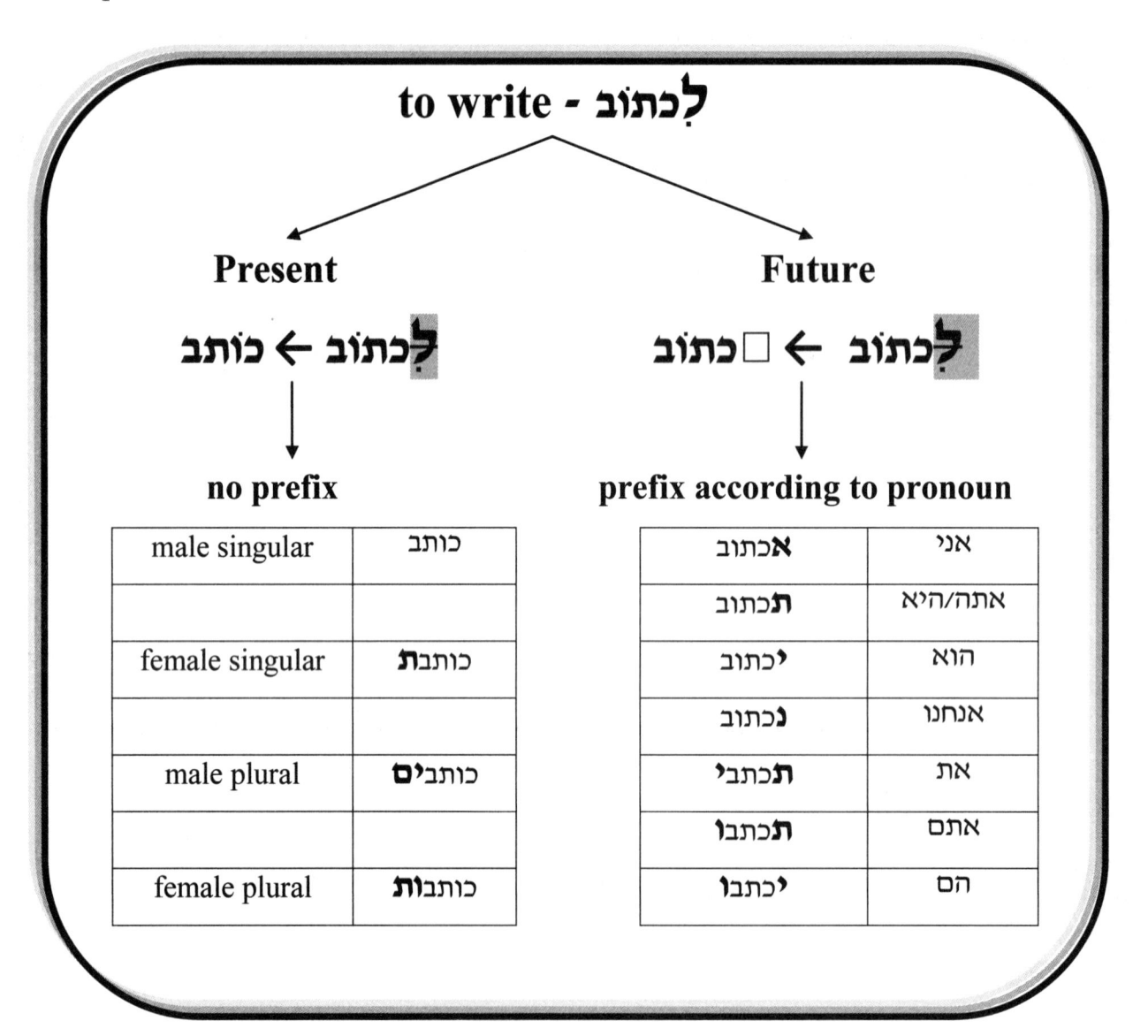

to write - לִכְתוֹב

Present: לִכְתוֹב ← כּוֹתֵב — no prefix

male singular	כותב
female singular	כותב**ת**
male plural	כותב**ים**
female plural	כותב**ות**

Future: לִכְתוֹב ← ☐כתוב — prefix according to pronoun

אני	**א**כתוב
אתה/היא	**ת**כתוב
הוא	**י**כתוב
אנחנו	**נ**כתוב
את	**ת**כתב**י**
אתם	**ת**כתב**ו**
הם	**י**כתב**ו**

Binyan Pa'al, Group 1, Subgroup 2

Reminder of the infinitive form of the Binyan

בניין פעל 1, תת-קבוצה 2

Infinitive form of each Binyan is the key to understanding the future tense structure. Let's review it now.

Infinitive Form

The infinitive form of subgroup 2 has the sound pattern:

LA...A...O...

*(A)...A...O... are the core sound patterns vowels

Example:

לַעֲבוֹד - to work

* The first vowel (A) is in parenthesis because it's part of the prefix sound

בניין פעל 1, תת-קבוצה 2

Binyan Pa'al, Group 1, Subgroup 2

Moving from Infinitive Form to Future Tense

In this group we omit the infinitive form prefix **לְ**, while maintaining the sound pattern of the infinitive form:

...A...A...O...

Instead of the **לְ** we use prefixes corresponding to the pronouns.

As an example let's use the verb to work – לַעֲבוֹד. Follow the arrows to find the prefixes used for each pronoun.

לַעֲבוֹד - to work

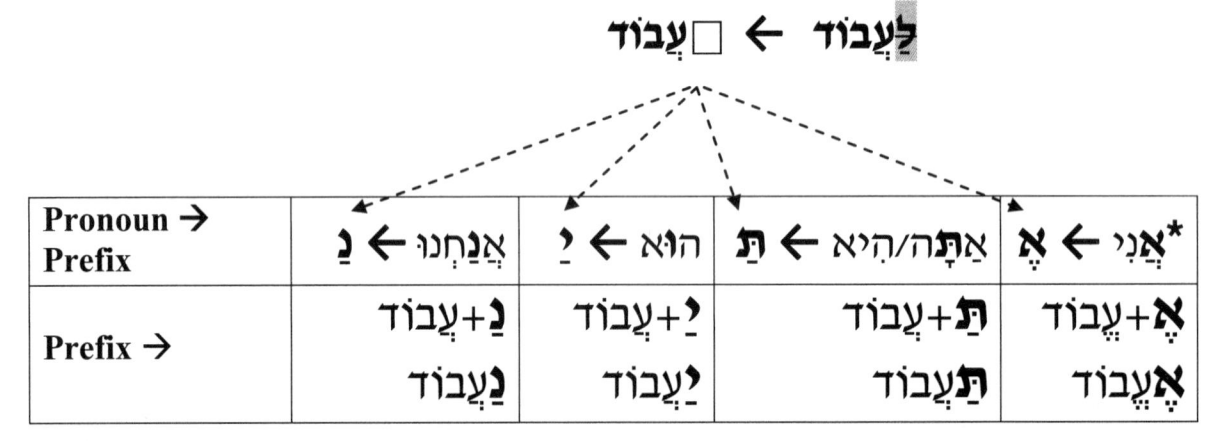

לַעֲבוֹד ← ☐ עֲבוֹד

Pronoun → Prefix	אֲנַחְנוּ ← נַ	הוּא ← יַ	אַתָּה/הִיא ← תַּ	*אֲנִי ← אֶ
Prefix →	נַ+עֲבוֹד נַעֲבוֹד	יַ+עֲבוֹד יַעֲבוֹד	תַּ+עֲבוֹד תַּעֲבוֹד	אֶ+עֲבוֹד אֶעֱבוֹד

As we add the corresponding suffixes, the 'O' sound disappears:

Pronoun → Prefix & Suffix	הֵם ← יַ+וּ	אַתֶּם ← תַּ+וּ	אַתְּ ← תַּ+י
Prefix & Suffix →	יַ+עַבְד+וּ יַעַבְדוּ	תַּ+עַבְד+וּ תַּעַבְדוּ	תַּ+עַבְד+י תַּעַבְדִי

*Note that the music for אֲנִי is "E..E..O..."

בניין פעל 1, תת-קבוצה 2

Moving from Infinitive Form to Future Tense

Starting with pronouns requiring only a prefix:

שם הפועל באנגלית	שֵׁם פֹּעַל Infinitive	אני	אתה/היא	הוא	אנחנו
to work	לַעֲבוֹד	אֶעֱבוֹד	תַּעֲבוֹד	יַעֲבוֹד	נַעֲבוֹד
to think	לַחֲשׁוֹב	אֶחֱשׁוֹב	תַּחְשׁוֹב	יַחְשׁוֹב	נַחְשׁוֹב
to return	לַחֲזוֹר	אֶחֱזוֹר	תַּחֲזוֹר	יַחֲזוֹר	נַחֲזוֹר
to stand	לַעֲמוֹד	אֶעֱמוֹד	תַּעֲמוֹד	יַעֲמוֹד	נַעֲמוֹד
to help	לַעֲזוֹר	אֶעֱזוֹר	תַּעֲזוֹר	יַעֲזוֹר	נַעֲזוֹר

Binyan Pa'al, Group 1, Subgroup 2

And now, pronouns which require a suffix as well:

הם	אתם	את	שֵׁם פֹּעַל Infinitive	שם הפועל באנגלית
יַעֲבְדוּ	תַּעֲבְדוּ	תַּעֲבְדִי	לַעֲבֹד	to work
יַחְשְׁבוּ	תַּחְשְׁבוּ	תַּחְשְׁבִי	לַחְשֹׁב	to think
יַחְזְרוּ	תַּחְזְרוּ	תַּחְזְרִי	לַחֲזֹר	to return
יַעַמְדוּ	תַּעַמְדוּ	תַּעַמְדִי	לַעֲמֹד	to stand
יַעַזְרוּ	תַּעַזְרוּ	תַּעַזְרִי	לַעֲזֹר	to help

Binyan Pa'al, Group 1, Subgroup 2

סִפּוּר: הַאִם הָרַכֶּבֶת תַּעֲזוֹר לָנוּ?

אוֹצַר מִלִּים

רַכֶּבֶת	train
הָרַכֶּבֶת הַקַּלָּה	light train
תַּחְשׁוֹב טוֹב – יִהְיֶה טוֹב	think good – it will be good
גְּאוּלָּה	redemption

סיפור: האם הרכבת תעזור לנו?

שלי: שרון, איזה כיף! הרכבת הקלה **תעבוד** באוגוסט.

שרון: אני קצת סקפטית. אני לא בטוחה שהיא באמת **תעבוד** באוגוסט הקרוב. אני לא בטוחה שהיא **תעבוד** גם באוגוסט הבא.

שלי: שרון, באמת! **תחשבי** טוב, יהיה טוב.

שרון: בסדר. **אחשוב** טוב, יהיה טוב. הרכבת **תעבוד** באוגוסט. אז מה?

שלי: אז מה?! אוי, שרון, יהיה טוב לנסוע ברכבת! טוב מאוד!

שרון: למה?

שלי: דבר ראשון, ברכבת יש הרבה הרבה מקום, וכולם יכולים לשבת. אנחנו לא **נעמוד** כל הדרך, כמו באוטובוס.

שרון: נכון. ברכבת באמת יש מקום לכולם, ואף אחד לא **יעמוד**. אבל...

שלי: דבר שני, הרכבת נוסעת יותר מהר מהאוטובוס. אני **אחזור** הביתה מהעבודה מהר, וגם את **תחזרי** הביתה מהעבודה מהר.

שרון: כן, זה נכון. כולם **יחזרו** הביתה מהר, אבל...

שלי: דבר שלישי, הרכבת גדולה, יפה ונעימה. הנהג **יעבוד** בשמחה, כל הנוסעים ירגישו טוב, וכולם **יעזרו** לכולם...

שרון: שלי, זו רק רכבת. זו לא הגאולה. וגם...

שלי: וגם מה? אבל מה? שרון, באמת! את לא מבינה כמה הרכבת **תעזור** לנו?

שרון: לא, אני לא מבינה, שלי. ואת יודעת למה הרכבת לא **תעזור** לנו?

שלי: למה?

שרון: דבר ראשון, כי הרכבת לא מגיעה למשרד שלנו, באולפן-אור. ודבר שני, כי את ואני הולכות תמיד ברגל.

Binyan Pa'al, Group 1, Subgroup 2

Now listen and read and check your comprehension sentence by sentence:

Shelley: Sharon, how great! The light train will work in August.	שלי: שרון, איזה כיף! הרכבת הקלה **תעבוד** באוגוסט.
Sharon: I'm a little skeptical. I'm not sure that it will really work this [close] August. I'm not sure it will work next August as well.	שרון: אני קצת סקפטית. אני לא בטוחה שהיא באמת **תעבוד** באוגוסט הקרוב. אני לא בטוחה שהיא **תעבוד** גם באוגוסט הבא.
Shelley: Sharon, really! Think good, it will be good.	שלי: שרון, באמת! **תחשבי** טוב, יהיה טוב.
Sharon: Okay. I'll think good, it will be good.	שרון: בסדר. **אחשוב** טוב, יהיה טוב.
The train will work in August. So what?	הרכבת **תעבוד** באוגוסט. אז מה?
Shelley: So what?! Oh, Sharon, it will be good to ride on the train! Very good!	שלי: אז מה?! אוי, שרון, יהיה טוב לנסוע ברכבת! טוב מאוד!
Sharon: Why?	שרון: למה?
Shelley: First [thing], on the train there is a lot [a lot] of room, and everyone can sit. We won't stand the whole way, like on the bus.	שלי: דבר ראשון, ברכבת יש הרבה הרבה מקום, וכולם יכולים לשבת. אנחנו לא **נעמוד** כל הדרך, כמו באוטובוס.
Sharon: Right. On the train there really is room for everyone, and no one will stand. But…	שרון: נכון. ברכבת באמת יש מקום לכולם, ואף אחד לא **יעמוד**. אבל…
Shelley: Second [thing], the train goes faster than the bus. I'll come back [return] home from work quickly,	שלי: דבר שני, הרכבת נוסעת יותר מהר מהאוטובוס. אני **אחזור** הביתה מהעבודה מהר,
and you'll come back home from work quickly as well.	וגם את **תחזרי** הביתה מהעבודה מהר.
Sharon: yes, that's true. Everyone will come back home quickly, but…	שרון: כן, זה נכון. כולם **יחזרו** הביתה מהר, אבל…
Shelley: Third [thing], the train is big, beautiful and pleasant. The driver will work happily,	שלי: דבר שלישי, הרכבת גדולה, יפה ונעימה. הנהג **יעבוד** בשמחה,

Binyan Pa'al, Group 1, Subgroup 2

all of the passengers will feel good, and everyone will help everyone…	כל הנוסעים ירגישו טוב, וכולם **יַעזרו** לכולם...
Sharon: Shelley, it's just a train. It's not [the] redemption. And also…	שרון : שלי, זו רק רכבת. זו לא הגאולה. וגם...
Shelley: And also what? But what? Sharon, really! Don't you understand how much the train will help us?	שלי : וגם מה? אבל מה? שרון, באמת! את לא מבינה כמה הרכבת **תעזור** לנו?
Sharon: No, I don't understand, Shelley. And do you know why the train won't help us?	שרון : לא, אני לא מבינה, שלי. ואת יודעת למה הרכבת לא **תעזור** לנו?
Shelley: Why?	שלי : למה?
Sharon: First [thing], because the train doesn't go [arrive] to our office, at Ulpan-Or. And second [thing], because you and I always walk [by foot].	שרון : דבר ראשון, כי הרכבת לא מגיעה למשרד שלנו, באולפן-אור. ודבר שני, כי את ואני הולכות תמיד ברגל.

Binyan Pa'al, Group 1, Subgroup 2

Check yourself

1. Tell the dialogue in Hebrew while reading the English text.

2. Fill in the right column in Hebrew and check yourself using the text on the previous page.

Shelley: Sharon, how great! The light train will work in August.	
Sharon: I'm a little skeptical. I'm not sure that it will really work this [close] August. I'm not sure it will work next August as well.	
Shelley: Sharon, really! Think good, it will be good.	
Sharon: Okay. I'll think good, it will be good.	
The train will work in August. So what?	
Shelley: So what?! Oh, Sharon, it will be good to ride on the train! Very good!	
Sharon: Why?	
Shelley: First [thing], on the train there is a lot [a lot] of room, and everyone can sit. We won't stand the whole way, like on the bus.	
Sharon: Right. On the train there really is room for everyone, and no one will stand. But…	
Shelley: Second [thing], the train goes faster than the bus. I'll come back [return] home from work quickly,	
and you'll come back home from work quickly as well.	
Sharon: yes, that's true. Everyone will come back home quickly, but…	

Binyan Pa'al, Group 1, Subgroup 2

Shelley: Third [thing], the train is big, beautiful and pleasant. The driver will work happily,	
all of the passengers will feel good, and everyone will help everyone…	
Sharon: Shelley, it's just a train. It's not [the] redemption. And also…	
Shelley: And also what? But what? Sharon, really! Don't you understand how much the train will help us?	
Sharon: No, I don't understand, Shelley. And do you know why the train won't help us?	
Shelley: Why?	
Sharon: First [thing], because the train doesn't go [arrive] to our office, at Ulpan-Or. And second [thing], because you and I always walk [by foot].	

Binyan Pa'al, Group 1, Subgroup 2

4. Create your own story

Your Story – Binyan Pa'al 1, Subgroup 2

Now create your own story in Hebrew using the above story as an example.

Use all or part of the following verbs in future tense:

work; think; return; stand; help

Binyan Pa'al, Group 1, Subgroup 2

בניין פעל 1, תת-קבוצה 2

Vocabulary Test

Complete the chart using the example:

הם	את	אתה/היא	אני	שֵׁם פֹּעַל Infinitive	שם הפועל באנגלית
יעבדו	**תעבדי**	תעבוד	אעבוד	לַעֲבוֹד	to work
					to think
					to return
					to stand
					to help

Binyan Pa'al, Group 1, Subgroup 2

6. Practice by creating and answering questions

Exercising Binyan Pa'al 1, Subgroup 2

Listen once to the following questions in order to practice verbs in this group. Then write the questions in Hebrew. Listen to the audio again and check your translation.

Questions	Hebrew Translation
1. Will you work next year? Where will you work?	
2. What will your friends think about your Hebrew?	
3. Will the Israelis stand in line quietly?	
4. When will you come back [return] home today?	
5. Who will always help you?	

Write your answers in Hebrew here:

1.

2.

3.

4.

5.

Binyan Pa'al, Group 1, Subgroup 2

Exercise: Fill in the missing parts in the chart. (You don't have to know the meaning of the verbs). Check yourself by listening to the CD.

Conjugation	Infinitive	Pronoun
תעצרו	לעצור stop	אַתֶּם
יהרוס	להרוס	הוּא
נעסוק	לעסוק	אֲנַחְנוּ
תחצוב	לחצוב	אַתָּה
תערבי	לערוב	אַתְּ
תהלום	להלום	הִיא
יחלקו	לחלוק divide/share	הֵם
אחפור	לחפור	אֲנִי

Binyan Pa'al, Group 1, Subgroup 2

Imperative Form of Binyan Pa'al 1, Subgroup 2

Let's use the future tense structure to create imperative form.

Remember: to create negative sentences the equivalent of **"Don't"** is אַל

Following are some examples of sentences using the imperative form:

| Help (m. sg.) me please. | תַּעֲזוֹר לִי בְּבַקָּשָׁה. |
| Don't stand (f. sg.) here, stand there! | אַל תַּעַמְדִי כָּאן, תַּעַמְדִי שָׁם! |

Exercise: Write your own sentences in English using verbs from Binyan Pa'al 1, Subgroup 2 in imperative form. Use both, negative and positive structures. Translate those to Hebrew in the table below:

English	Hebrew

Binyan Pa'al, Group 1, Subgroup 2

Summary of Binyan Pa'al 1, Subgroup 2
Present and Future Tense

Notice how the basic sound of the Binyan remains the same, as only the suffixes and prefixes alternate.

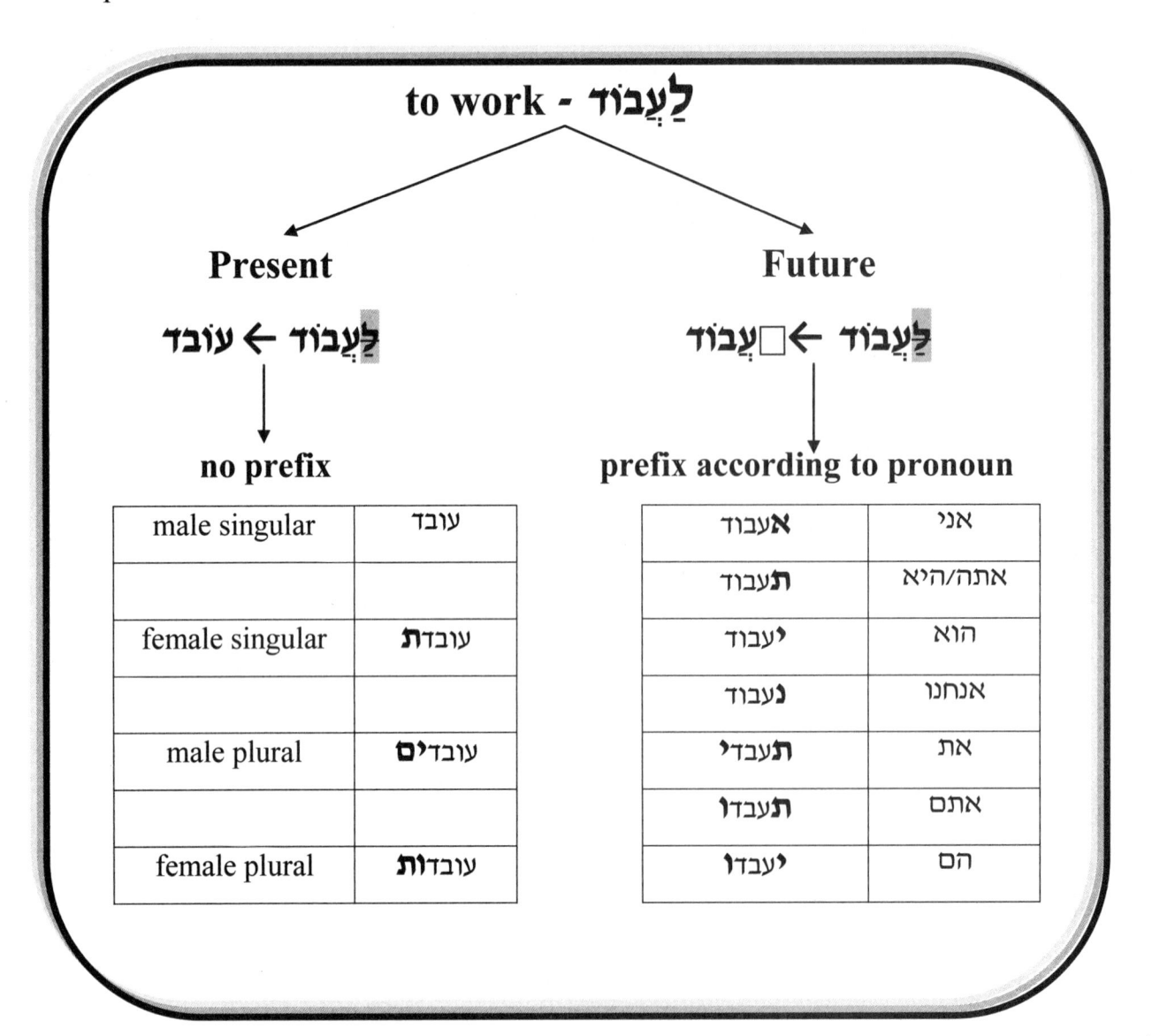

לַעֲבוֹד - to work

Present

לַעֲבוֹד ← עוֹבֵד

no prefix

male singular	עובד
female singular	עובד**ת**
male plural	עובד**ים**
female plural	עובד**ות**

Future

לַעֲבוֹד ← ❒עֱבוֹד

prefix according to pronoun

אני	**א**עבוד
אתה/היא	**ת**עבוד
הוא	**י**עבוד
אנחנו	**נ**עבוד
את	**ת**עבד**י**
אתם	**ת**עבד**ו**
הם	**י**עבד**ו**

CD2 Track 20

Binyan Pa'al, Group 1, Subgroup 3

Reminder of the infinitive form of the Binyan

בניין פעל 1, תת-קבוצה 3

Infinitive form of each Binyan is the key to understanding the future tense structure. Let's review it now.

Infinitive Form

The infinitive form of subgroup 3 has the sound pattern:

lA...E...Et

*(A)...E...E... are the core sound pattern vowels

Example:

To walk, to go - לָלֶכֶת

* The first vowel (A) is in parenthesis because it's part of the prefix sound

Binyan Pa'al, Group 1, Subgroup 3

בניין פעל 1, תת-קבוצה 3

Moving from Infinitive Form to Future Tense

In this group we omit the infinitive form prefix לְ, as well as the ending ת. So the sound pattern is:

...E...E...

Instead of the לְ we use prefixes corresponding to the pronouns. As an example let's use the verb to walk, to go – לָלֶכֶת. Follow the arrows to find the prefixes used for each pronoun.

to walk, to go - לָלֶכֶת

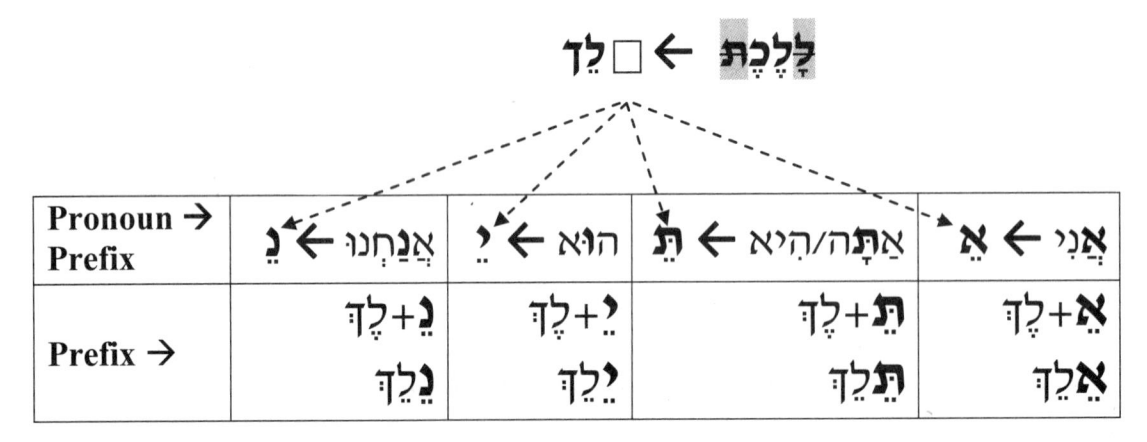

לָלֶכֶת ← לֶ☐

Pronoun → Prefix	אֲנַחְנוּ ← נֶ	הוּא ← יֶ	אַתָּה/הִיא ← תֶּ	אֲנִי ← אֶ
Prefix →	נֶ+לֵךְ נֵלֵךְ	יֶ+לֵךְ יֵלֵךְ	תֶּ+לֵךְ תֵּלֵךְ	אֶ+לֵךְ אֵלֵךְ

As we add the corresponding suffixes, the 'E' sound disappears:

Pronoun → Prefix & Suffix →	הֵם ← יֶ+וּ	אַתֶּם ← תֶּ+וּ	אַתְּ ← תֶּ+י
Prefix & Suffix →	יֶ+לכ+וּ יֵלְכוּ	תֶּ+לכ+וּ תֵּלְכוּ	תֶּ+לכ+י תֵּלְכִי

Binyan Pa'al, Group 1, Subgroup 3

2. Practice conversion to future tense

בניין פעל 1, תת-קבוצה 3

Moving from Infinitive Form to Future Tense

Starting with pronouns requiring only a prefix:

אנחנו	הוא	אתה/היא	אני	שֵׁם פֹּעַל Infinitive	שם הפועל באנגלית
נֵלֵךְ	יֵלֵךְ	תֵּלֵךְ	אֵלֵךְ	לָלֶכֶת	to walk
נֵשֵׁב	יֵשֵׁב	תֵּשֵׁב	אֵשֵׁב	לָשֶׁבֶת	to sit
נֵרֵד	יֵרֵד	תֵּרֵד	אֵרֵד	לָרֶדֶת	to go down
נֵצֵא	יֵצֵא	תֵּצֵא	אֵצֵא	לָצֵאת	to get out
נִיתֵּן	יִתֵּן	תִּיתֵּן	אֶתֵּן	*לָתֵת לָתֵת	to give

*Notice that **לתת** is an irregular verb. In the future tense a final letter "Nun" **'ן'** is added at the end of the verb.
Except for the first person, it has different music in the future tense - EE...E...

Binyan Pa'al, Group 1, Subgroup 3

Only for אֲנִי the music remains E...E...

And now, pronouns which require a suffix as well:

שֵׁם הפועל באנגלית	שֵׁם פֹּעַל Infinitive	את	אתם	הם
to walk	לָלֶכֶת	תֵּלְכִי	תֵּלְכוּ	יֵלְכוּ
to sit	לָשֶׁבֶת	תֵּשְׁבִי	תשבו	ישבו
to go down	לָרֶדֶת	תֵּרְדִי	תרדו	ירדו
to get out	לָצֵאת	תֵּצְאִי	תצאו	יצאו
*to give	*לָתֵת	תִּתְּנִי	תִּתְּנוּ	יִתְּנוּ

*Pay attention again to the verb לתת, which has a slightly different sound pattern in the future tense.

סִפּוּר: לְאָן נֵצֵא בְּיוֹם הַהוּלֶדֶת?

אוֹצַר מִלִּים

לָרֶדֶת לְאֵילַת	to go (down) to Eilat
לָשֶׁבֶת בְּמִסְעָדָה	to sit in a restaurant
חוּפְשַׁת הַקַּיִץ (הַחוֹפֶשׁ הַגָּדוֹל)	summer break
קְחוּ אֶת הַזְּמַן	take the (your) time (pl.)

אמא: ענת, היום יום ההולדת שלך. אולי **נצא** יחד?

ענת: כן, למה לא? לאן **נצא**?

אמא: אולי **נלך** למוזיאון?

ענת: אמא, באמת, אני לא **אלך** למוזיאון. אולי אבא **ילך** איתך למוזיאון, ביום-ההולדת שלך.

אמא: טוב, אז לאן **נלך**?

ענת: אולי **נשב** במסעדה הכי יקרה בירושלים?

אמא: במסעדה הכי יקרה בירושלים? ומי ישלם?

ענת: ממם... שאלה טובה. טוב, אולי לא **נשב** במסעדה.

אמא: אז לאן **נלך**?

ענת: אולי **נרד** לאילת ל-3 ימים?

אמא: איך **ארד** לאילת ל-3 ימים? אני עובדת מחר! ואיך את **תרדי** לאילת? את לומדת מחר!

ענת: מה הבעיה? אני לא **אלך** לבית הספר, ואת לא **תלכי** לעבודה.

אמא: ענתי, באמת. את יודעת שאי אפשר לרדת לאילת עכשיו. אבל בחופשת הקיץ, את והחברות שלך **תרדו** יחד, בסדר?

ענת: בסדר. ועכשיו, לאן **נצא**?

אמא: ממם... אולי **נלך** לסרט?

ענת: אני לא יודעת. אני לא אוהבת את הסרטים שלך ושל אבא. אה, אני יודעת!

אמא: מה?

ענת: את ואבא **תצאו** יחד. **תלכו** לסרט, **תלכו** למוזיאון, **תשבו** במסעדה... קחו את הזמן. ואני אשאר בבית לבד ואזמין את כל הכיתה שלי למסיבת יום הולדת. מה את אומרת?

Binyan Pa'al, Group 1, Subgroup 3

סִפּוּר: לְאָן נֵצֵא בְּיוֹם הַהוּלֶדֶת?

Now listen and read and check your comprehension sentence by sentence:

Mom: Anat, today is your birthday. Maybe we should [will] go out together?	אמא: ענת, היום יום ההולדת שלך. אולי **נצא** יחד?
Anat: Yes, why not? Where will we go out to?	ענת: כן, למה לא? לאן **נצא**?
Mom: Maybe we'll go to a museum?	אמא: אולי **נלך** למוזיאון?
Anat: Mom, really, I won't go to a museum. Maybe dad will go with you to a museum, on your birthday.	ענת: אמא, באמת, אני לא **אלך** למוזיאון. אולי אבא **ילך** איתך למוזיאון, ביום-ההולדת שלך.
Mom: Okay, so where will we go?	אמא: טוב, אז לאן **נלך**?
Anat: Maybe we'll sit at the most expensive restaurant in Jerusalem?	ענת: אולי **נשב** במסעדה הכי יקרה בירושלים?
Mom: At the most expensive restaurant in Jerusalem? And who will pay (for it)?	אמא: במסעדה הכי יקרה בירושלים? ומי ישלם?
Anat: Hmm... good question. Okay, maybe we won't sit in a restaurant.	ענת: מממ... שאלה טובה. טוב, אולי לא **נשב** במסעדה.
Mom: So where will we go to?	אמא: אז לאן **נלך**?
Anat: Maybe we'll go [down] to Eilat for 3 days?	ענת: אולי **נרד** לאילת ל-3 ימים?
Mom: How will I go [down] to Eilat for 3 days? I'm working tomorrow! And how will you go to Eilat? You're studying tomorrow!	אמא: איך **ארד** לאילת ל-3 ימים? אני עובדת מחר! ואיך את **תרדי** לאילת? את לומדת מחר!
Anat: What's the problem? I won't go to school, and you won't go to work.	ענת: מה הבעיה? אני לא **אלך** לבית הספר, ואת לא **תלכי** לעבודה.
Mom: Anati, really. You know that (it's) impossible to go to Eilat now. But in the summer break you and your friends will go together, okay?	אמא: ענתי, באמת. את יודעת שאי אפשר לרדת לאילת עכשיו. אבל בחופשת הקיץ, את והחברות שלך **תרדו** יחד, בסדר?

Binyan Pa'al, Group 1, Subgroup 3

Anat: Okay. And now? Where will we go out to?	ענת: בסדר. ועכשיו, לאן **נצא**?
Mom: Hmm… maybe we'll go to a movie?	אמא: ממממ... אולי **נלך** לסרט?
Anat: I don't know. I don't like your and dad's movies. Ah, I know!	ענת: אני לא יודעת. אני לא אוהבת את הסרטים שלך ושל אבא. אה, אני יודעת!
Mom: What?	אמא: מה?
Anat: You and dad will go out together.	ענת: את ואבא **תצאו** יחד.
You'll go to a movie, [will] go to a museum, [will] sit in a restaurant… take your [the] time. And I'll stay home alone and invite all of my class to a birthday party. What do you say?	**תלכו** לסרט, **תלכו** למוזיאון, **תשבו** במסעדה... קחו את הזמן. ואני אֶשָׁאֵר בבית לבד וַאֲזמין את כל הכיתה שלי למסיבת יום הולדת. מה את אומרת?

Binyan Pa'al, Group 1, Subgroup 3

Check yourself

1. Tell the dialogue in Hebrew while reading the English text.
2. Fill in the right column in Hebrew and check yourself using the text on the previous page.

Mom: Anat, today is your birthday. Maybe we should [will] go out together?	
Anat: Yes, why not? Where will we go out to?	
Mom: Maybe we'll go to a museum?	
Anat: Mom, really, I won't go to a museum. Maybe dad will go with you to a museum, on your birthday.	
Mom: Okay, so where will we go?	
Anat: Maybe we'll sit at the most expensive restaurant in Jerusalem?	
Mom: At the most expensive restaurant in Jerusalem? And who will pay (for it)?	
Anat: Hmm… good question. Okay, maybe we won't sit in a restaurant.	
Mom: So where will we go to?	
Anat: Maybe we'll go [down] to Eilat for 3 days?	
Mom: How will I go [down] to Eilat for 3 days? I'm working tomorrow! And how will you go to Eilat? You're studying tomorrow!	
Anat: What's the problem? I won't go to school, and you won't go to work.	

Binyan Pa'al, Group 1, Subgroup 3

Mom: Anati, really. You know that (it's) impossible to go to Eilat now. But in the summer break you and your friends will go together, okay?	
Anat: Okay. And now? Where will we go out to?	
Mom: Hmm… maybe we'll go to a movie?	
Anat: I don't know. I don't like your and dad's movies. Ah, I know!	
Mom: What?	
Anat: You and dad will go out together.	
You'll go to a movie, [will] go to a museum, [will] sit in a restaurant… take your [the] time. And I'll stay home alone and invite all of my class to a birthday party. What do you say?	

Binyan Pa'al, Group 1, Subgroup 3

4. Create your own story

Your Story – Binyan Pa'al 1, Subgroup 3

Now create your own story in Hebrew using the above story as an example.

Use all or part of the following verbs in future tense:

walk/go; sit; go down; get out/go out; give

בניין פעל 1, תת-קבוצה 3

Vocabulary Test

Complete the chart according to the example:

הם	את	אתה/היא	אני	שֵׁם פֹּעַל Infinitive	שם הפועל באנגלית
יֵלכו	תֵלכי	תֵלך	אֵלך	לָלֶכֶת	to walk
					to sit
					to go down
					to get out
					to give

CD2 Track 24

Binyan Pa'al, Group 1, Subgroup 3

6. Practice by creating and answering questions

Exercising Binyan Pa'al 1, Subgroup 3

Listen once to the following questions in order to practice verbs in this group. Then write the questions in Hebrew. Listen to the audio again and check your translation.

Questions	Hebrew Translation
1. Where will you go today? Who will you go with?	
2. At which restaurant will you and your friends sit?	
3. In your city, will a lot of rain come down at winter? And when it will rain, will you go out or will you stay [at] home?	
4. When will you go out of the house tomorrow?	
5. What will you give your friend for (his) birthday? What will he give you?	

Write your answers here:

1.

2.

3.

4.

5.

אולפן-אור

Copyrighted and owned by Ulpan-Or. Any usage without express permission from Ulpan-Or is prohibited.
כל הזכויות שמורות לאולפן-אור. כל שימוש, העתקה והפצה אסורים.

Binyan Pa'al, Group 1, Subgroup 3

Exercise: Fill in the missing parts in the chart. (You don't have to know the meaning of the verbs). Check yourself by listening to the CD.

Conjugation	Infinitive	Pronoun
נושאים	לשאת	אַתֶּם
יושב	לשבת	הוּא
יורד	לרדת	אֲנַחְנוּ
תצא	לצאת	אַתָּה
תלכי	ללכת	אַתְּ
תיתן	לתת	הִיא
ירדו	לרדת	הֵם
אלד	ללדת to give birth	אֲנִי

Binyan Pa'al, Group 1, Subgroup 3

Imperative Form of Binyan Pa'al 1, Subgroup 3

Let's use the future tense structure to create imperative form.

Remember: to create negative sentences the equivalent of **"Don't"** is אַל.

Following are some examples of sentences using the imperative form:

Get off (pl. m.) the bus quickly!	תֵּרְדוּ מֵהָאוֹטוֹבּוּס מַהֵר!
Don't give (f. sg.) him this book!	אַל תִּתְּנִי לוֹ אֶת הַסֵּפֶר הַזֶּה!

Exercise: Write your own sentences in English using verbs from Binyan Pa'al 1, Subgroup 3 in imperative form. Use both, negative and positive structures. Translate those to Hebrew in the table below:

English	Hebrew

Binyan Pa'al, Group 1, Subgroup 3

Summary of Binyan Pa'al 1, Subgroup 3
Present and Future Tense

Notice how the basic sound of the Binyan remains the same, as only the suffixes and prefixes alternate.

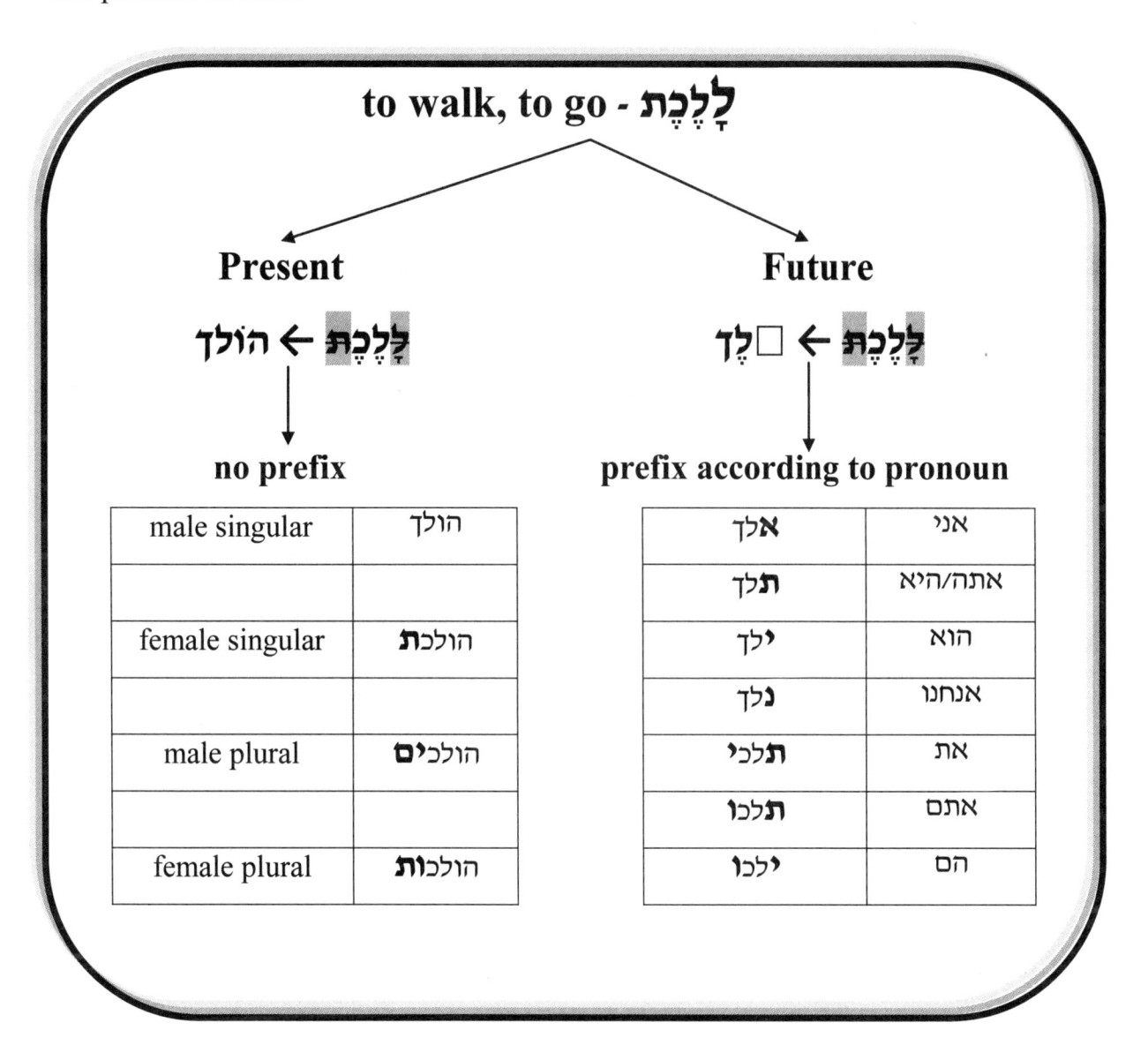

to walk, to go - לָלֶכֶת

Present

לָלֶכֶת → הוֹלֵךְ

no prefix

male singular	הולך
female singular	הולכת
male plural	הולכים
female plural	הולכות

Future

לָלֶכֶת → לֵךְ □

prefix according to pronoun

אני	**א**לך
אתה/היא	**ת**לך
הוא	**י**לך
אנחנו	**נ**לך
את	**ת**לכי
אתם	**ת**לכו
הם	**י**לכו

		Reminder of the infinitive form of the Binyan
CD3 Track 1	Binyan Pa'al, Group 1, Subgroup 4	

בניין פעל 1, תת-קבוצה 4

Infinitive form of each Binyan is the key to understanding the future tense structure. Let's review it now.

Infinitive Form

The infinitive form of subgroup 4 has the sound pattern:

lEE...O...A

*(EE)...O...A are the core sound pattern vowels

Example:

to hear - לִשְׁמוֹעַ

* The first vowel (EE) is in parenthesis because it's part of the prefix sound

בניין פעל 1, תת-קבוצה 4

Moving from Infinitive Form to Future Tense

In this group we omit the infinitive form prefix ל, and the middle sound O.

The sound pattern changes from EE...O...A to EE...A:

...EE...O̸...A ⟹ ...EE...A

Instead of the ל we use prefixes corresponding to the pronouns.

As an example let's use the verb to hear – לִשְׁמוֹעַ. Follow the arrows to find the prefixes used for each pronoun.

to hear - לִשְׁמוֹעַ

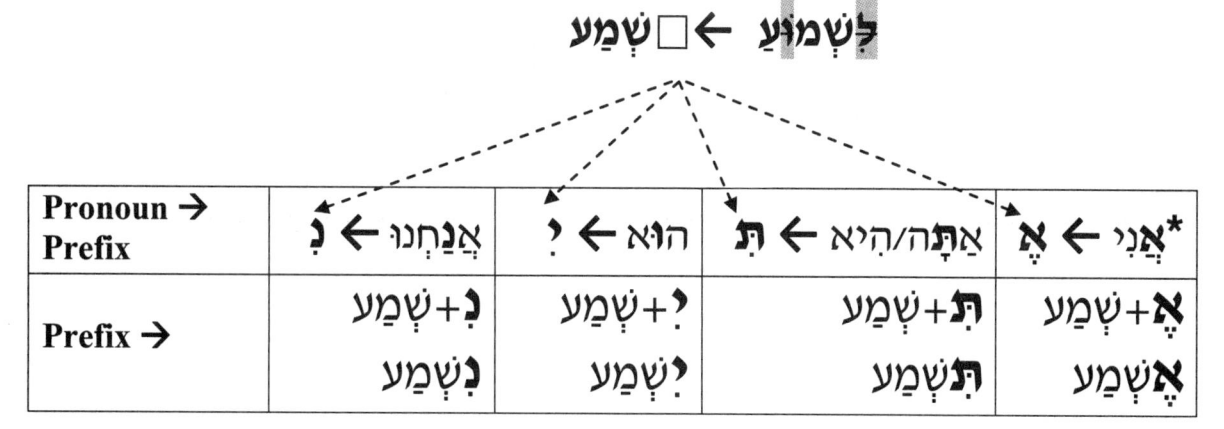

לִשְׁמוֹעַ ← □שְׁמַע

Pronoun → Prefix	אֲנַחְנוּ ← נ	הוּא ← י	אַתָּה/הִיא ← תּ	*אֲנִי ← אֶ
Prefix →	נ+שְׁמַע נִשְׁמַע	י+שְׁמַע יִשְׁמַע	תּ+שְׁמַע תִּשְׁמַע	אֶ+שְׁמַע אֶשְׁמַע

As we add the corresponding suffixes, the 'A' sound disappears:

Pronoun → Prefix & Suffix	הֵם ← י+וּ	אַתֶּם ← תּ+וּ	אַתְּ ← תּ+י
Prefix & Suffix →	י+שְׁמְע+וּ יִשְׁמְעוּ	תּ+שְׁמְע+וּ תִּשְׁמְעוּ	תּ+שְׁמְע+י תִּשְׁמְעִי

*Note that the music for אֲנִי is "E...A..."

Binyan Pa'al, Group 1, Subgroup 4

בניין פעל 1, תת-קבוצה 4

Moving from Infinitive Form to Future Tense

2. Practice conversion to future tense

Starting with pronouns requiring only a prefix:

אנחנו	הוא	אתה/היא	אני	שֵׁם פֹּעַל Infinitive	שם הפועל באנגלית
נִשְׁמַע	יִשְׁמַע	תִּשְׁמַע	אֶשְׁמַע	לִשְׁמוֹעַ	to hear, to listen
נקבע	יקבע	תקבע	אקבע	לִקְבּוֹעַ	to set (a meeting)
נִיסַּע	יִסַּע	תִּיסַּע	אֶסַּע	*לִנְסוֹעַ	*to travel, to go

*Note: in the verb **לנסוע**, the letter **נ** is dropped out in the future tense.

Binyan Pa'al, Group 1, Subgroup 4

And now, pronouns which require a suffix as well:

שֵׁם הפועל באנגלית	שֵׁם פֹּעַל Infinitive	אַת	אַתֶם	הם
to hear, to listen	לִשְׁמוֹעַ	תִּשְׁמְעִי	תִּשְׁמְעוּ	יִשְׁמְעוּ
to set (a meeting)	לִקְבּוֹעַ	תִּקְבְּעִי	תִּקְבְּעוּ	יִקְבְּעוּ
*to travel, to go	*לִנְסוֹעַ	תִּסְעִי	תִּסְעוּ	יִסְעוּ

*Note: in the verb **לנסוע**, the letter **נ** is dropped out in the future tense.

Binyan Pa'al, Group 1, Subgroup 4

סִפּוּר: מִבְחָן בְּהִיסְטוֹרְיָה

אוֹצַר מִלִּים

מִבְחָן	test
אַחֵר	different
בִּמְקוֹם	instead of
לְהַצְלִיחַ (הִפְעִיל)	to succeed

המורה: תלמידים, שקט בבקשה. **תשמעו**, ביום חמישי הבא יש לכם מבחן בהיסטוריה.

תלמידה: ביום חמישי הבא? לא, זה לא טוב! אולי **נקבע** יום אחר?

המורה: למה? מה הבעיה?

תלמידה: ביום רביעי בערב יש לי מסיבת יום הולדת.

המורה: אוי, באמת. אז **תקבעי** את המסיבה ליום חמישי בערב. אנחנו לא **נקבע** יום אחר בגלל יום ההולדת שלך, נכון? טוב, יש עוד בעיות או שאלות?

תלמידה: כן, המורה. אולי במקום מבחן בהיסטוריה, **ניסע** לטיול בירושלים? ירושלים עיר מאוד היסטורית.

המורה: אם כולם יצליחו במבחן, אולי **ניסע** לטיול בירושלים, בסדר? ועכשיו, מספיק עם השאלות. בהצלחה!

Binyan Pa'al, Group 1, Subgroup 4

Now listen and read and check your comprehension sentence by sentence:

Teacher: Students, quiet please. Listen [hear], on next Thursday you have a history test.	מורה: תלמידים, שקט בבקשה. **תשמעו**, ביום חמישי הבא יש לכם מבחן בהיסטוריה.
Student: Next Thursday? No, it's not good. Maybe we'll set a different day?	תלמידה: ביום חמישי הבא? לא, זה לא טוב! אולי **נקבּע** יום אחר?
Teacher: Why? What's the problem?	מורה: למה? מה הבעיה?
Student: On Wednesday night I have a birthday party.	תלמידה: ביום רביעי בערב יש לי מסיבת יום הולדת.
Teacher: Oh, really. So set the party for Thursday night. We won't set a different day because of your birthday, right? Okay, are there (any) more problems or questions?	מורה: אוי, באמת. אז **תקבעי** את המסיבה ליום חמישי בערב. אנחנו לא **נקבּע** יום אחר בגלל יום ההולדת שלך, נכון? טוב, יש עוד בעיות או שאלות?
Student: Yes, teacher. Maybe instead of a history test, we'll go for a trip in Jerusalem?	תלמידה: כן, המורה. אולי בּמקום מבחן בהיסטוריה, **ניסע** לטיול בירושלים?
Jerusalem is a very historic city.	ירושלים עיר מאוד היסטורית.
Teacher: If everyone (will) succeed in the test, maybe we'll go for a trip in Jerusalem, okay? And now, enough with the questions. Good luck!	מורה: אם כולם יצליחו במבחן, אולי **ניסע** לטיול בירושלים, בסדר? ועכשיו, מספיק עם השאלות. בהצלחה!

Binyan Pa'al, Group 1, Subgroup 4

Check yourself

1. Tell the dialogue in Hebrew while reading the English text.

2. Fill in the right column in Hebrew and check yourself using the text on the previous page.

Teacher: Students, quiet please. Listen [hear], on next Thursday you have a history test.	
Student: Next Thursday? No, it's not good. Maybe we'll set a different day?	
Teacher: Why? What's the problem?	
Student: On Wednesday night I have a birthday party.	
Teacher: Oh, really. So set the party for Thursday night. We won't set a different day because of your birthday, right? Okay, are there (any) more problems or questions?	
Student: Yes, teacher. Maybe instead of a history test, we'll go for a trip in Jerusalem?	
Jerusalem is a very historic city.	
Teacher: If everyone will succeed in the test, maybe we'll go for a trip in Jerusalem, okay? And now, enough with the questions. Good luck!	

Binyan Pa'al, Group 1, Subgroup 4

4. Create your own story

Your Story – Binyan Pa'al 1, Subgroup 4

Now create your own story in Hebrew using the above story as an example.

Use all or part of the following verbs in future tense:

hear/listen; set; go

Binyan Pa'al, Group 1, Subgroup 4

5. Take a vocabulary test

בניין פעל 1, תת-קבוצה 4

Vocabulary Test

Complete the chart:

הם	את	אתה/היא	אני	שֵׁם פֹּעַל Infinitive	שם הפועל באנגלית
ישמעו	תשמעי	תשמע	אשמע	לִשְׁמֹעַ	to hear, to listen
					to set (a meeting)
					to travel, to go

Exercising Binyan Pa'al 1, Subgroup 4

Listen once to the following questions in order to practice verbs in this group. Then write the questions in Hebrew. Listen to the audio again and check your translation.

Questions	Hebrew Translation
1. In ten years, which music will most of the people in the world hear?	
2. Who will set a meeting with you?	
3. Where will your family go to in the summer?	

Write your answers in Hebrew here:

.1

.2

.3

Binyan Pa'al, Group 1, Subgroup 4

Exercise: Fill in the missing parts in the chart. (You don't have to know the meaning of the verbs). Check yourself by listening to the CD.

Conjugation	Infinitive	Pronoun
תצבעו	לצבוע	אַתֶּם
יברח	לברוח	הוּא
נקלע	לקלוע	אֲנַחְנוּ
תצלח	לצלוח	אַתָּה
תצלחי תתמהי	לתמוה	אַתְּ
תצמח	לצמוח	הִיא
יבלעו	לבלוע	הֵם
אגבה אגבה	לגבוה	אֲנִי

Binyan Pa'al, Group 1, Subgroup 4

Imperative Form of Binyan Pa'al 1, Subgroup 4

Let's use the future tense structure to create imperative form.

Remember: to create negative sentences the equivalent of **"Don't"** is אַל.

Following are some examples of sentences using the imperative form:

Don't set up (f. sg.) appointments for tomorrow.	אַל תִּקְבְּעִי פְּגִישׁוֹת לְמָחָר.
Listen (m. sg.) to me!	תִּשְׁמַע לִי!

Exercise: Write your own sentences in English using verbs from Binyan Pa'al 1, Subgroup 4 in imperative form. Use both, negative and positive structures. Translate those to Hebrew in the table below:

English	Hebrew

Binyan Pa'al, Group 1, Subgroup 4

Summary of Binyan Pa'al 1, Subgroup 4
Present and Future Tense

Notice how the basic sound of the Binyan remains the same, as only the suffixes and prefixes alternate.

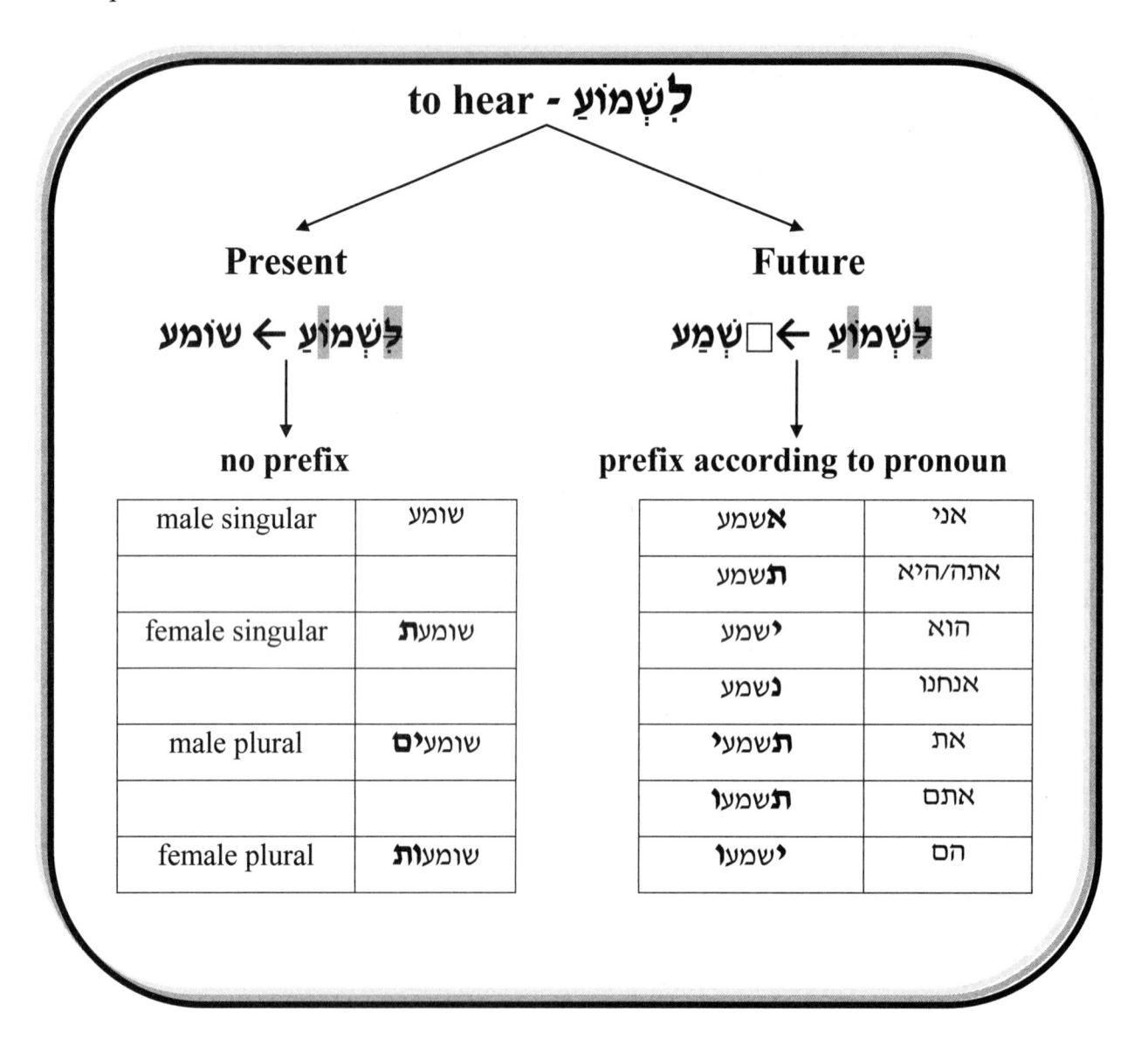

לִשְׁמוֹעַ - to hear

Present

שׁוֹמֵעַ ← לִשְׁמוֹעַ

no prefix

male singular	שומע
female singular	שומע**ת**
male plural	שומע**ים**
female plural	שומע**ות**

Future

שְׁמַע☐ ← לִשְׁמוֹעַ

prefix according to pronoun

אני	**א**שמע
אתה/היא	**ת**שמע
הוא	**י**שמע
אנחנו	**נ**שמע
את	**ת**שמעי
אתם	**ת**שמעו
הם	**י**שמעו

CD3 Track 7

Binyan Pa'al, Group 1, Subgroup 5

Reminder of the infinitive form of the Binyan

בניין פעל 1, תת-קבוצה 5

Infinitive form of each Binyan is the key to understanding the future tense structure. Let's review it now.

Infinitive form

The infinitive form of subgroup 5 has the sound pattern:

LA...A...AT

*(A)...A...A... are the core sound pattern vowels

Example:

לָקַחַת - to take

* The first vowel (A) is in parenthesis because it's part of the prefix sound

Binyan Pa'al, Group 1, Subgroup 5

בניין פעל 1, קבוצה 5

Moving from Infinitive Form to Future Tense

In this group we omit the infinitive form prefix **לְ**, and also the suffix **ת**. The sound pattern changes from A…A… to:

…I…A… or to …E…A…

Instead of the **לְ** we use prefixes corresponding to the pronouns.

As an example let's use the verb to take – לָקַחַת. Follow the arrows to find the prefixes used for each pronoun.

to take - לָקַחַת

לָקַחַת ← קַח □

Pronoun → Prefix	*אֲנִי ← אֶ	אַתָּה/הִיא ← תִּ	הוּא ← יִ	אֲנַחְנוּ ← נִ
Prefix →	אֶ+קַח אֶקַח	תִּ+קַח תִּקַח	יִ+קַח יִקַח	נִ+קַח נִקַח

As we add the corresponding suffixes, the 'A' sound disappears:

Pronoun → Prefix & Suffix →	אַתְּ ← תִּ+י	אַתֶּם ← תִּ+וּ	הֵם ← יִ+וּ
Prefix & Suffix →	תִּ+קְח+י תִּקְחִי	תִּ+קְח+וּ תִּקְחוּ	יִ+קְח+וּ יִקְחוּ

*Note that the music for אֲנִי is "E..A..."

פעל 1, תת-קבוצה 5

Moving from Infinitives to Future Tense

Starting with pronouns requiring only a prefix:

אנחנו	הוא	אתה/היא	אני	שֵׁם פֹּעַל Infinitive	שם הפועל באנגלית
נִיקַח	יִקַח	תִיקַח	אֶקַח	לָקַחַת	to take
נִגַּע	יִגַּע	תִגַּע	אֶגַּע	לָגַעַת	to touch
נֵדַע	יֵדַע	תֵדַע	אֵדַע	*לָדַעַת	*to know

*Notice that the sound pattern for **לדעת** is "E...A..." in all of the pronouns, same as the music for the pronoun **אני**.

Binyan Pa'al, Group 1, Subgroup 5

And now, pronouns which require a suffix as well:

הם	אתם	את	שֵׁם פֹּעַל Infinitive	שם הפועל באנגלית
יִקְחוּ	תִּקְחוּ	תִּקְחִי	לָקַחַת	to take
יִגְּעוּ	תִּגְּעוּ	תִּגְּעִי	לָגַעַת	to touch
יֵדְעוּ	תֵּדְעוּ	תֵּדְעִי	*לָדַעַת	*to know

*Notice that the sound pattern for **לדעת** is "E…☐…" for all of the pronouns, as opposed to "EE…☐…" in other verbs.

Binyan Pa'al, Group 1, Subgroup 5

סִפּוּר: הָעוּגָה שֶׁל אִמָּא

אוֹצַר מִלִּים

smell something smells good!	רֵיחַ אֵיזֶה רֵיחַ טוֹב!
bite to take a bite	בִּיס לָקַחַת בִּיס

דן: ממממ... אמא, איזה ריח טוב יש מהמטבח! מה יש שם?

אמא: במטבח? אה.... אין שם כלום.

דן: מה כלום? יש שם עוגה. אני רואה שם עוגת שוקולד! אני הולך לאכול!

אמא: לא! אל **תיגע** בעוגה! דודה חיה ודוד חיים באים היום לביקור, והעוגה בשבילם.

דן: בסדר, אז **אקח** רק ביס קטן.

אמא: אל **תיקח** ביס - לא גדול ולא קטן!

דן: נו, אמא, רק ביס קטן... הדודים לא **יידעו**.

אמא: דודה חיה **תדע**. היא תמיד יודעת הכל.

דן: טוב, טוב, אני לא **אגע** בעוגה. אבל אולי הכלב שלנו **ייגע** בה...

אמא: דן, אני אומרת שוב - אל **תיגע** בעוגה!

דן: לא, לא אני. אבל אולי החתולה שלנו **תיגע** בה...

אמא: דן! אם **תיקח** ביס עכשיו, לא אתן לך לאכול עוגת שוקולד כל השנה.

דן: טוב, טוב, לא **אקח**. דודה חיה ודוד חיים **ייקחו** הכל, הם הכי חשובים. אני? אני רק הבן שלך. אני יכול ללכת לישון רעב.

Binyan Pa'al, Group 1, Subgroup 5

Now listen and read and check your comprehension sentence by sentence:

Dan: Hmm… Mom, something smells good from the kitchen! What's over there?	דן : ממממ... אמא, איזה ריח טוב יש מהמטבח! מה יש שם?
Mom: In the kitchen? Ah… There's nothing there.	אמא : במטבח? אה.... אין שם כלום.
Dan: What (do you mean) nothing? There's a cake there. I see a chocolate cake there! I'm going to eat (it)!	דן : מה כלום? יש שם עוגה. אני רואה שם עוגת שוקולד! אני הולך לאכול!
Mom: No! Don't touch the cake! Aunt Chaya and uncle Chayim are coming today for a visit, and the cake is for them.	אמא : לא! אל **תיגע** בעוגה! דודה חיה ודוד חיים באים היום לביקור, והעוגה בשבילם.
Dan: Okay, so I'll take just a little bite.	דן : בסדר, אז **אקח** רק ביס קטן.
Mom: Don't take a bite – not big and not small!	אמא : אל **תיקח** ביס - לא גדול ולא קטן!
Dan: Come on, mom, just a little bite… The aunt and uncle won't know.	דן : נו, אמא, רק ביס קטן... הדודים לא **יידעו**.
Mom: Aunt Chaya will know. She always knows everything.	אמא : דודה חיה **תדע**. היא תמיד יודעת הכל.
Dan: Okay, okay, I won't touch the cake. But maybe our dog will touch it…	דן : טוב, טוב, אני לא **אגע** בעוגה. אבל אולי הכלב שלנו **ייגע** בה...
Mom: Dan, I'm saying again – don't touch the cake!	אמא : דן, אני אומרת שוב - אל **תיגע** בעוגה!
Dan: No. not me. But maybe our cat will touch it…	דן : לא, לא אני. אבל אולי החתולה שלנו **תיגע** בה...
Mom: Dan! If you take a bite now, I won't let you eat chocolate cake all year (round).	אמא : דן! אם **תיקח** ביס עכשיו, לא אתן לך לאכול עוגת שוקולד כל השנה.
Dan: Okay, okay, I won't take (any).	דן : טוב, טוב, לא **אקח**.
Aunt Chaya and uncle Chayim will take everything, they are the most important. Me? I'm just your son. I can go to sleep hungry.	דודה חיה ודוד חיים **ייקחו** הכל, הם הכי חשובים. אני? אני רק הבן שלך. אני יכול ללכת לישון רעב.

Binyan Pa'al, Group 1, Subgroup 5

Check yourself

1. Tell the dialogue in Hebrew while reading the English text.

2. Fill in the right column in Hebrew and check yourself using the text on the previous page.

Dan: Hmm… Mom, something smells good from the kitchen! What's over there?	
Mom: In the kitchen? Ah… There's nothing there.	
Dan: What (do you mean) nothing? There's a cake there. I see a chocolate cake there! I'm going to eat (it)!	
Mom: No! Don't touch the cake! Aunt Chaya and uncle Chayim are coming today for a visit, and the cake is for them.	
Dan: Okay, so I'll take just a little bite.	
Mom: Don't take a bite – not big and not small!	
Dan: Come on, mom, just a little bite… The aunt and uncle won't know.	
Mom: Aunt Chaya will know. She always knows everything.	
Dan: Okay, okay, I won't touch the cake.	
But maybe our dog will touch it…	
Mom: Dan, I'm saying again – don't touch the cake!	
Dan: No. not me. But maybe our cat will touch it…	
Mom: Dan! If you take a bite now, I won't let you eat chocolate cake all year (round).	
Dan: Okay, okay, I won't take (any).	
Aunt Chaya and uncle Chayim will take everything, they are the most important. Me? I'm just your son. I can go to sleep hungry.	

Binyan Pa'al, Group 1, Subgroup 5

Your Story – Binyan Pa'al 1, Subgroup 5

Now create your own story in Hebrew using the above story as an example.

Use all or part of the following verbs in future tense:

know; touch; take

4. Create your own story

Binyan Pa'al, Group 1, Subgroup 5

בניין פעל 1, תת-קבוצה 5

Vocabulary Test

5. Take a vocabulary test

Complete the chart:

הם	את	אתה/היא	אני	שֵׁם פֹּעַל Infinitive	שם הפועל באנגלית
יקחו	תיקחי	תיקח	אקח	לָקַחַת	to take
					to touch
					to know

Exercising Binyan Pa'al 1, Subgroup 5

Listen to the following questions. Then write the questions from English to Hebrew. Check yourself by listening to the audio again.

Questions	Hebrew Translation
1. Do you believe that you'll touch the stars?	
2. Will it take you a lot of time to get home today?	
3. Will we know everything one day? What will we never know?	

Write your answers in Hebrew here:

.1

.2

.3

Binyan Pa'al, Group 1, Subgroup 5

Exercise: Fill in the missing parts in the chart. (You don't have to know the meaning of the verbs). Check yourself by listening to the CD.

Conjugation	Infinitive	Pronoun
תִּגְּעוּ	לגעת	אַתֶּם
יִקַּח	לקחת	הוּא
נֵדַע	לדעת	אֲנַחְנוּ
תִּטַּע	לטעת	אַתָּה
תִּקְּחִי	לקחת	אַתְּ
תִּטַּע	לטעת	הִיא
יִגְּעוּ	לגעת	הֵם
אֵדַע	לדעת	אֲנִי

Binyan Pa'al, Group 1, Subgroup 5

Imperative Form of Binyan Pa'al 1, Subgroup 5

Let's use the future tense structure to create imperative form.

Remember: to create negative sentences the equivalent of **"Don't"** is אַל

Following are some examples of sentences using the imperative form:

Don't touch (m. sg.) it!	!אַל תִּיגַּע בְּזֶה
Take (f. sg.) the dog with you!	!תִּקְחִי אֶת הַכֶּלֶב אִיתָּךְ

Exercise: Write your own sentences in English using verbs from Binyan Pa'al 1, Subgroup 5 in imperative form. Use both, negative and positive structures. Translate those to Hebrew in the table below:

English	Hebrew

Binyan Pa'al, Group 1, Subgroup 5

Summary of Binyan Pa'al 1, Subgroup 5
Present and Future Tense

Notice how the basic sound of the Binyan remains the same, as only the suffixes and prefixes alternate.

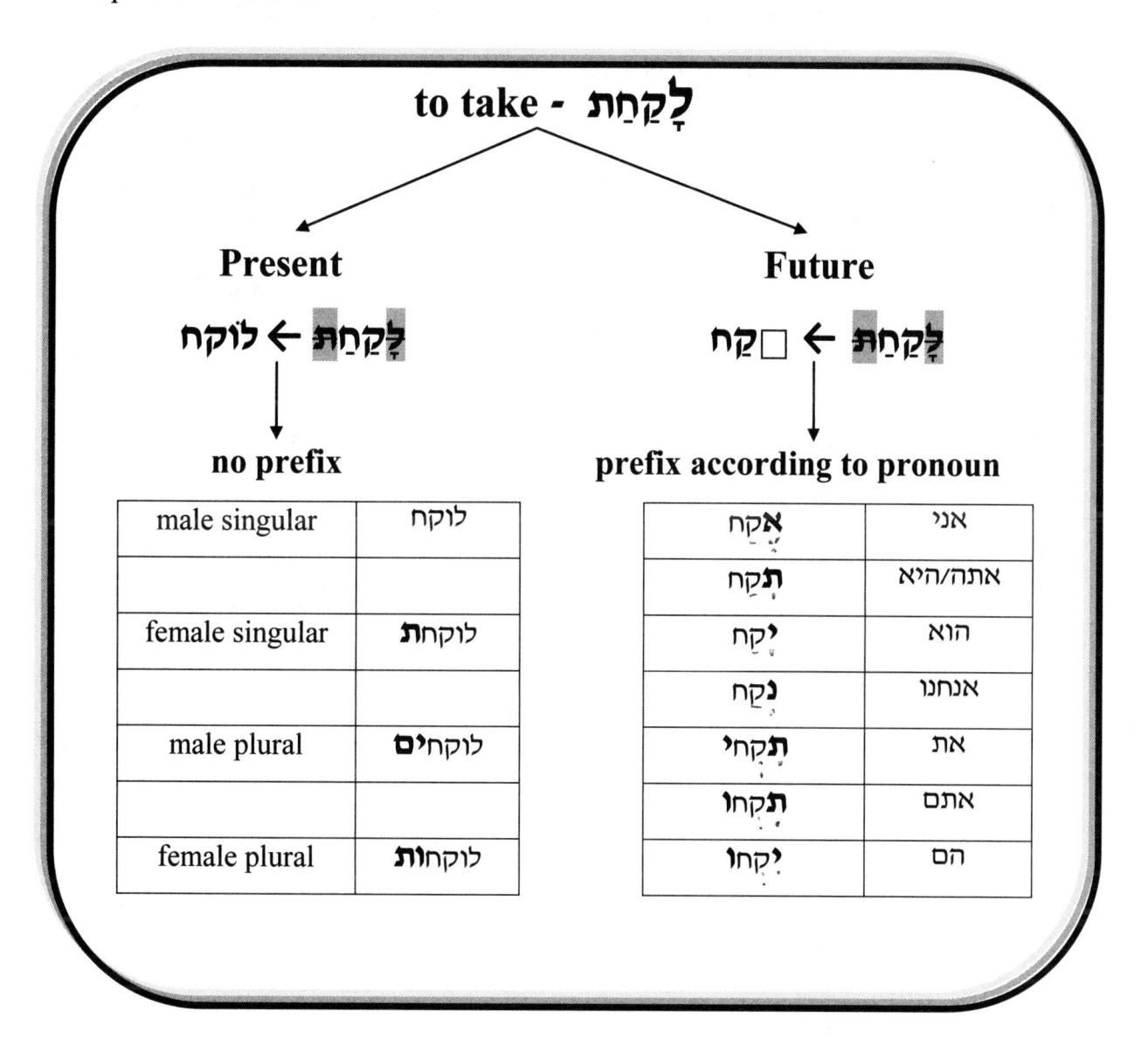

to take - לָקַחַת

Present

לָקַחַת ← לוֹקֵח

no prefix

male singular	לוֹקֵח
female singular	לוֹקַחַת
male plural	לוֹקְחִים
female plural	לוֹקְחוֹת

Future

לָקַחַת ← קַח☐

prefix according to pronoun

אני	**אֶ**קַח
אתה/היא	**תִּ**קַח
הוא	**יִ**קַח
אנחנו	**נִ**קַח
את	**תִּ**קְחִי
אתם	**תִּ**קְחוּ
הם	**יִ**קְחוּ

Binyan Pa'al, Group 1, Subgroup 6

Reminder of the infinitive form of the Binyan

בניין פעל 1, תת-קבוצה 6

Infinitive form of each Binyan is the key to understanding the future tense structure. Let's review it now.

Infinitive form

The infinitive form of subgroup 6 has the following sound pattern:

LE...E...O...

*(E)...E...O... are the core sound pattern vowels

Example:

to eat - לֶאֱכֹל

* The first vowel (E) is in parenthesis because it's part of the prefix sound

בניין פעל 1, תת-קבוצה 6
Moving from Infinitive Form to Future Tense

In this group we omit the infinitive form prefix לְ, and the sound pattern changes from E...O... to:

...O...A...

Instead of the לְ we use prefixes corresponding to the pronouns.

As an example let's use the verb to eat - לֶאֱכֹל. Follow the arrows to find the prefixes used for each pronoun.

to eat - לֶאֱכֹל

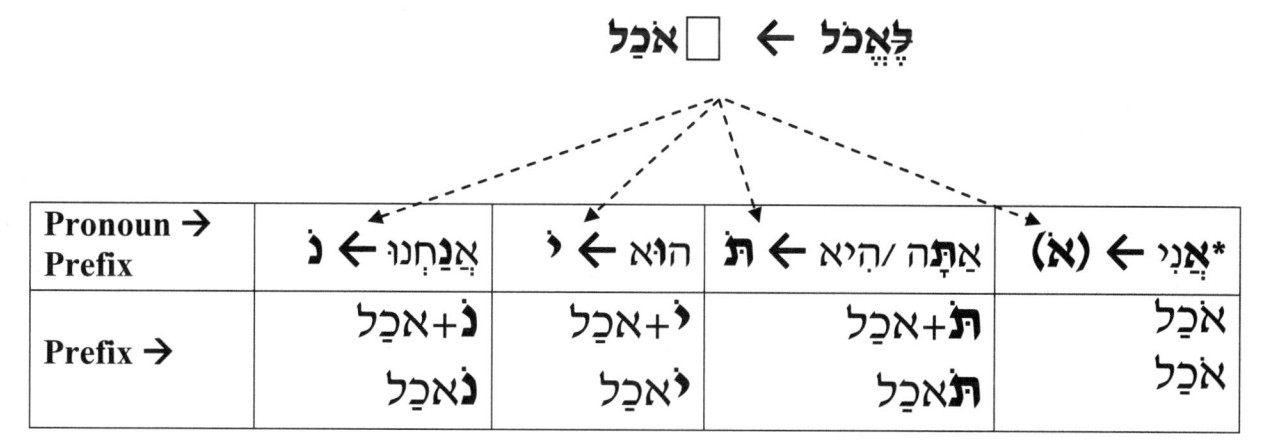

לֶאֱכֹל ← אֹכַל □

Pronoun → Prefix	אֲנַחְנוּ ← נ	הוּא ← י	אַתָּה/הִיא ← תּ	*אֲנִי ← (א)
Prefix →	נ+אכַל נֹאכַל	י+אכַל יֹאכַל	תּ+אכַל תֹּאכַל	אֹכַל אֹכַל

As we add the corresponding suffixes, the 'A' sound disappears:

Pronoun → Prefix & Suffix	הֵם ← י + וּ	אַתֶּם ← תּ + וּ	אַתְּ ← תּ + י
Prefix & Suffix →	י+אכְל+וּ יֹאכְלוּ	תּ+אכְל+וּ תֹּאכְלוּ	תּ+אכְל+י תֹּאכְלִי

* **Pay attention:** For the first person the prefix א and the first root letter א just coincide.

Moving from Infinitive Form to Future Tense

בניין פעל 1, תת-קבוצה 6

Binyan Pa'al, Group 1, Subgroup 6

Starting with pronouns requiring only a prefix:

שם הפועל באנגלית	שֵׁם פֹּעַל Infinitive	אני	אתה/היא	הוא	אנחנו
to love, to like	לֶאֱהֹב	אֹהַב	תֹּאהַב	יֹאהַב	נֹאהַב
to eat	לֶאֱכֹל	אֹכַל	תֹּאכַל	יֹאכַל	נֹאכַל
*to say	*לוֹמַר	אֹמַר	תֹּאמַר	יֹאמַר	נֹאמַר

*Notice that the infinitive לוֹמַר has a different sound pattern. Its original (biblical) pattern was לֶאֱמֹר, and so it conjugates the same as the rest of the group.

Binyan Pa'al, Group 1, Subgroup 6

And now, pronouns which require a suffix as well:

הם	אתם	את	שֵׁם פֹּעַל Infinitive	שם הפועל באנגלית
יֹאהֲבוּ	תֹּאהֲבוּ	תֹּאהֲבִי	לֶאֱהֹב	to love, to like
יֹאכְלוּ	תֹּאכְלוּ	תֹּאכְלִי	לֶאֱכֹל	to eat
יֹאמְרוּ	תֹּאמְרוּ	תֹּאמְרִי	לוֹמַר	to say

סִפּוּר: תָּכְנִית רִיאָלִיטִי

אוֹצַר מִלִּים

truth	אֱמֶת
to take part, to participate	לְהִשְׁתַּתֵּף (הִתְפַּעֵל)
(TV) show	תָּכְנִית
slang: to beat someone easily (lit. to eat someone without salt)	לֶאֱכוֹל (מִישֶׁהוּ) בְּלִי מֶלַח
angry (f. sg.)	כּוֹעֶסֶת

דנה: שירה, אני רוצה לשאול אותך משהו, אבל **תאמרי** לי את האמת.

שירה: בסדר. **אומר** לך רק את האמת.

דנה: יופי. אני רוצה להשתתף בתוכנית ריאליטי. מה את אומרת?

שירה: להשתתף בתוכנית ריאליטי? באיזו תוכנית ריאליטי?

דנה: ממממ... אני לא יודעת. אולי ב"מאסטר שף"? כן, ב"מאסטר שף". אני אבשל וכולם **יאכלו** את האוכל שלי- בטלוויזיה!

שירה: אממממ... אני לא יודעת, דנה. אני לא בטוחה שכולם **יאכלו** את האוכל שלך. את לא יודעת לבשל, את זוכרת?

דנה: כן, נכון. אני באמת לא יודעת לבשל. טוב, אז אולי "באח הגדול"?

שירה: "האח הגדול"? מה פתאום, דנה! את כל כך נחמדה ונאיבית. האנשים "באח הגדול" **יאכלו** אותך בלי מלח.

דנה: טוב, אז... אולי ב"אמריקן איידול"? כן, אני חושבת שאני רוצה להשתתף ב"אמריקן איידול". אני כל כך אוהבת לשיר, ובטח **אוהב** לשיר עם המוזיקאים של "אמריקן איידול".

שירה: כן, את בטח **תאהבי** לשיר עם המוזיקאים של "אמריקן איידול", אבל אני לא בטוחה שהמוזיקאים **יאהבו** לשמוע אותך... את מבינה, דנה, את לא ממש יודעת לשיר.

דנה: שירה, באמת! את אומרת שאני נאיבית, שאני לא יודעת לשיר, שאני לא יודעת לבשל... אולי **תאמרי** לי משהו נחמד?

שירה: אני לא מבינה, דנה, למה את כועסת? את לא רוצה **שאומר** לך את האמת?

דנה: כן, אני רוצה **שתאמרי** לי את האמת. אבל רק אמת נחמדה, שכיף לשמוע.

Binyan Pa'al, Group 1, Subgroup 6

Now listen and read and check your comprehension sentence by sentence:

Dana: Shira, I want to ask you something, but tell me the truth.	דנה: שירה, אני רוצה לשאול אותך משהו, אבל **תֹּאמְרִי** לי את האמת.
Shira: Okay. I'll only tell you the truth.	שירה: בסדר. **אוֹמַר** לך רק את האמת.
Dana: Good. I want to take part in a reality show. What do you say?	דנה: יופי. אני רוצה להשתתף בתוכנית ריאליטי. מה את אומרת?
Shira: To take part in a reality show? In which reality show?	שירה: להשתתף בתוכנית ריאליטי? באיזו תוכנית ריאליטי?
Dana: Hmm... I don't know. Maybe on 'Master Chef'? Yes, on 'Master Chef'. I'll cook and everyone will eat my food – on TV!	דנה: ממממ.. אני לא יודעת. אולי ב"מאסטר שף"? כן, ב"מאסטר שף". אני אֲבַשֵּׁל וכולם **יֹאכְלוּ** את האוכל שלי- בטלוויזיה!
Shira: Hmm... I don't know, Dana. I'm not sure that everyone will eat your food. You don't know (how) to cook, remember?	שירה: אממממ.. אני לא יודעת, דנה. אני לא בטוחה שכולם **יֹאכְלוּ** את האוכל שלך. את לא יודעת לבשל, את זוֹכֶרֶת?
Dana: Yeah, right. I really don't know (how) to cook. Okay, so maybe on 'Big Brother'?	דנה: כן, נכון. אני באמת לא יודעת לבשל. טוב, אז אולי "באח הגדול"?
Shira: 'Big Brother'? no way, Dana! You are so nice and naïve. The people on 'Big Brother' will beat you easily (lit. will eat you without salt).	שירה: "האח הגדול"? מה פתאום, דנה! את כל כך נחמדה ונאיבית. האנשים "באח הגדול" **יֹאכְלוּ** אותך בלי מלח.
Dana: Okay, so... maybe on 'American Idol'? Yes, I think I want to take part in 'American Idol'.	דנה: טוב, אז... אולי ב"אמריקן איידול"? כן, אני חושבת שאני רוצה להשתתף ב"אמריקן איידול".
I love to sing so much, and I will surely love to sing with the musicians of 'American Idol'.	אני כל כך אוהבת לשיר, ובטח **אוֹהַב** לשיר עם המוזיקאים של "אמריקן איידול".
Shira: Yes, you will surely love to sing with the musicians of 'American Idol', but I'm not sure that the musicians will love to hear you...	שירה: כן, את בטח **תֹּאהֲבִי** לשיר עם המוזיקאים של "אמריקן איידול", אבל אני לא בטוחה שהמוזיקאים **יֹאהֲבוּ** לשמוע אותך...
You [understand] see, Dana, you don't really know (how) to sing.	את מבינה, דנה, את לא ממש יודעת לשיר.
Dana: Shira, really! You say that I'm naïve, that I don't know (how) sing, that I don't know (how) to cook... maybe you should say something nice to me?	דנה: שירה, באמת! את אומרת שאני נאיבית, שאני לא יודעת לשיר, שאני לא יודעת לבשל... אולי **תֹּאמְרִי** לי משהו נחמד?
Shira: I don't understand, Dana, why are you angry? You don't want me to tell you the truth?	שירה: אני לא מבינה, דנה, למה את כועסת? את לא רוצה שֶ**אוֹמַר** לך את האמת?
Dana: yes, I want you to tell me the truth. But only fun truth, that's fun to hear.	דנה: כן, אני רוצה שֶ**תֹּאמְרִי** לי את האמת. אבל רק אמת נחמדה, שכיף לשמוע.

Binyan Pa'al, Group 1, Subgroup 6

Check yourself

1. Tell the dialogue in Hebrew while reading the English text.
2. Fill in the right column in Hebrew and check yourself using the text on the previous page.

Dana: Shira, I want to ask you something, but tell me the truth.	
Shira: Okay. I'll only tell you the truth.	
Dana: Good. I want to take part in a reality show. What do you say?	
Shira: To take part in a reality show? In which reality show?	
Dana: Hmm... I don't know. Maybe on 'Master Chef'? Yes, on Master Chef: I'll cook and everyone would eat my food – on TV!	
Shira: Hmm... I don't know, Dana. I'm not sure that everyone would eat your food. You don't know (how) to cook, remember?	
Dana: Yeah, right. I really don't know (how) to cook. Okay, so maybe on 'Big Brother'?	
Shira: 'Big Brother'? no way, Dana! You are so nice and naïve. The people on 'Big Brother' will beat you easily (lit. will eat you without salt).	
Dana: Okay, so... maybe on 'American Idol'? Yes, I think I want to take part in 'American Idol'.	
I love to sing so much, and I will surely love to sing with the musicians of 'American Idol'.	
Shira: Yes, you will surely love to sing with the musicians of 'American Idol', but I'm not sure that the musicians will love to hear you...	
You see [understand], Dana, you don't really know (how) to sing.	
Dana: Shira, really! You say that I'm naïve, that I can't sing, that I can't cook... maybe you should say something nice to me?	
Shira: I don't understand, Dana, why are you angry? You don't want me to tell you the truth?	
Dana: yes, I want you to tell me the truth. But only fun truth, that's fun to hear.	

Binyan Pa'al, Group 1, Subgroup 6

4. Create your own story

Your Story – Binyan Pa'al 1, Subgroup 6

Now create your own story in Hebrew using the above story as an example.

Use all or part of the following verbs in future tense:

eat, love, say

בניין פעל 1, תת-קבוצה 6

Vocabulary Test

Complete the chart:

הם	את	אתה/היא	אני	שֵׁם פֹּעַל Infinitive	שם הפועל באנגלית
יאהבו	תאהבי	תאהב	אוהב	לֶאֱהֹב	to love, to like
					to eat
					to say

Exercising Binyan Pa'al 1, Subgroup 6

Listen to the following questions. Then write the questions from English to Hebrew. Check yourself by listening to the audio again.

Questions	Hebrew Translation
1. What will you (m.) eat for breakfast?	
2. When will the Israelis eat barbeque? (מַנְגָּל)	
3. How will you (m.) say in Hebrew "I want to visit Israel?	
4. Will the Chinese (סִינִים) like falafel?	

Write your answers in Hebrew here:

.1

.2

.3

.4

Binyan Pa'al, Group 1, Subgroup 6

Exercise: Fill in the missing parts in the chart. (You don't have to know the meaning of the verbs). Check yourself by listening to the CD.

Conjugation	Infinitive	Pronoun
אוֹכְלִים	לאכול	אַתֶּם
אוֹהֵב	לאהוב	הוּא
אוֹמְרִים	לומר	אֲנַחְנוּ
אוֹהֵב	לאהוב	אַתָּה
אוֹכֶלֶת	לאכול	אַתְּ
אוֹכֶלֶת	לאכול	הִיא
אוֹמְרִים	לומר	הֵם
אוֹהֶבֶת	לאהוב	אֲנִי

Binyan Pa'al, Group 1, Subgroup 6

Imperative Form of Binyan Pa'al 1, Subgroup 6

Let's use the future tense structure to create imperative form.

Remember: to create negative sentences the equivalent of **"Don't"** is **אַל**

Following are some examples of sentences using the imperative form:

Don't eat (pl. m.) dinner at home, we will eat in a restaurant.	אַל תֹּאכְלוּ אֶת אֲרוּחַת הָעֶרֶב בַּבַּיִת, נֹאכַל בְּמִסְעָדָה.
Tell (m. sg.) me, how old are you?	תֹּאמַר לִי, בֶּן כַּמָּה אַתָּה?

Exercise: Write your own sentences in English using verbs from Binyan Pa'al 1, Subgroup 6 in imperative form. Use both, negative and positive structures. Translate those to Hebrew in the table below:

English	Hebrew

Binyan Pa'al, Group 1, Subgroup 6

Summary of Binyan Pa'al 1, Subgroup 6
Present and Future Tense

Notice how the basic sound of the Binyan remains the same, as only the suffixes and prefixes alternate.

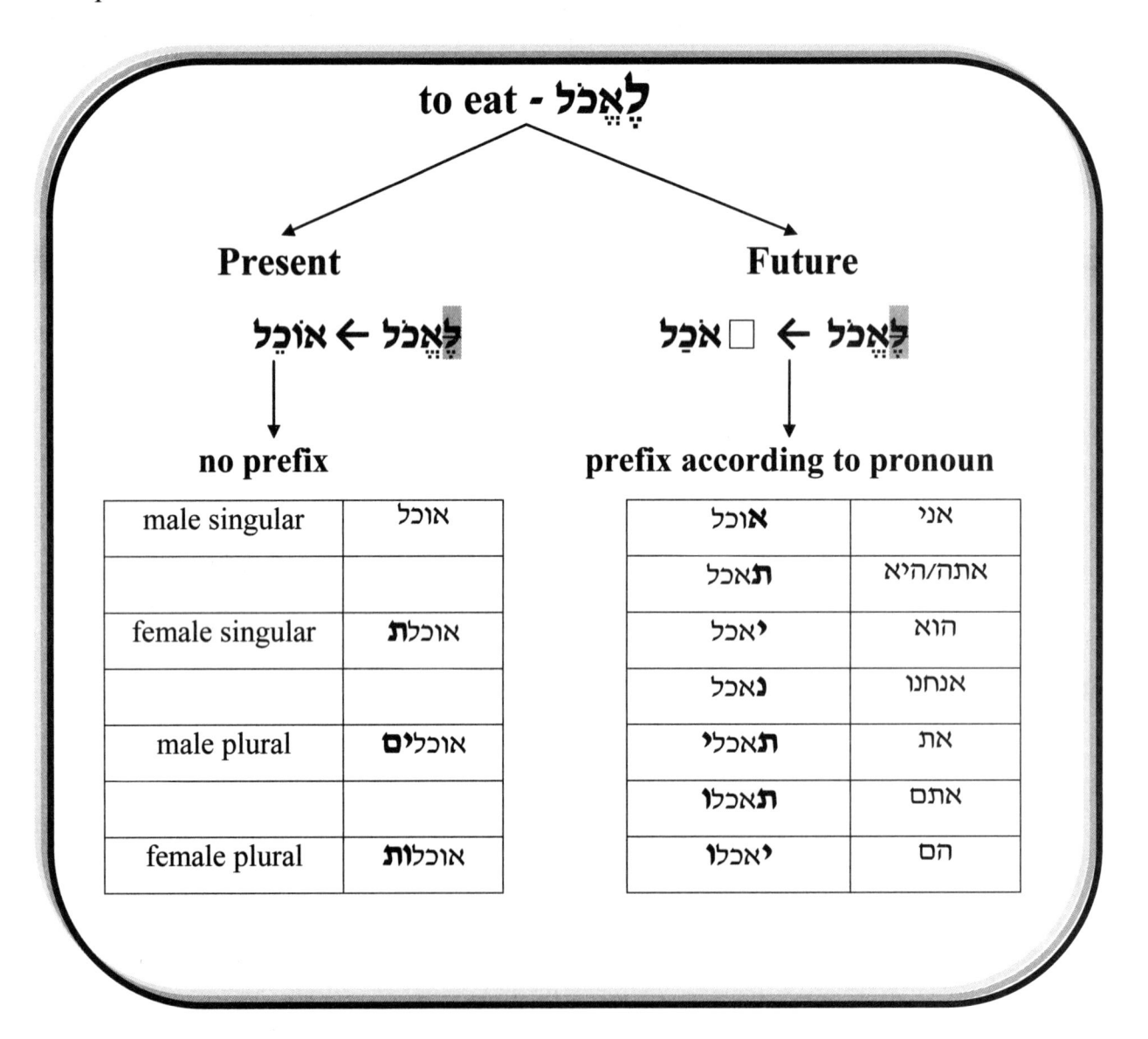

to eat - לֶאֱכֹל

Present
לֶאֱכֹל ← אוֹכֵל

no prefix

male singular	אוכל
female singular	אוכל**ת**
male plural	אוכל**ים**
female plural	אוכל**ות**

Future
לֶאֱכֹל ← אֹכַל □

prefix according to pronoun

אני	**א**וכל
אתה/היא	**ת**אכל
הוא	**י**אכל
אנחנו	**נ**אכל
את	**ת**אכלי
אתם	**ת**אכלו
הם	**י**אכלו

CD3 Track 19

Binyan Pa'al, Group 2

Reminder of the infinitive form of the Binyan

בניין פעל, קבוצה 2

Infinitive form of each Binyan is the key to understanding the future tense structure. Let's review it now.

Infinitive Form

The infinitive form of Binyan Pa'al 2, has the following sound pattern:

LA...(vowel = OU or O)...

*(A)...OU   or   *(A)...O are the core sound pattern vowels

Example:

to live - לָגוּר

to come - לָבוֹא

* The first vowel **(A)** is in parenthesis because it's part of the prefix sound

Binyan Pa'al, Group 2

בניין פעל, קבוצה 2

1. Learn the structure of the Binyan in future tense

Moving from Infinitive Form to Future Tense

In Pa'al 2 we omit the infinitive form prefix לָ, while maintaining the sound pattern of the infinitive form

…A…(vowel = OU, EE, O)…

Instead of the לָ we use prefixes corresponding to the pronouns.

As an example let's use the verb to live - לָגוּר. Follow the arrows to find the prefixes used for each pronoun.

to live / to reside - לָגוּר

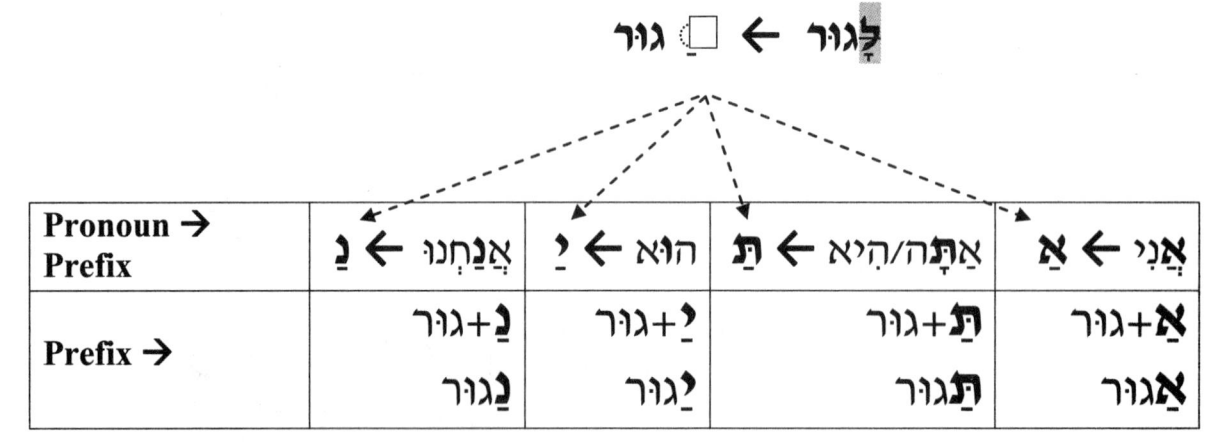

לָגוּר ← גוּר ☐

Pronoun → Prefix	אֲנַחְנוּ ← נַ	הוּא ← יַ	אַתָּה/הִיא ← תַ	אֲנִי ← אַ
Prefix →	נַ+גוּר נַגוּר	יַ+גוּר יַגוּר	תַ+גוּר תַגוּר	אַ+גוּר אַגוּר

Now we will also need to add the corresponding suffixes:

Pronoun → Prefix & Suffix	הֵם ← יַ+וּ	אַתֶּם ← תַ+וּ	אַתְּ ← תַ+י
Prefix & Suffix →	יַ+גוּר+וּ יַגוּרוּ	תַ+גוּר+וּ תַגוּרוּ	תַ+גוּר+י תַגוּרִי

בניין פעל, קבוצה 2

Binyan Pa'al, Group 2

Moving from Infinitive Form to Future Tense

Starting with pronouns requiring only a prefix:

אנחנו	הוא	אתה/היא	אני	שֵׁם פֹּעַל Infinitive	שם הפועל באנגלית
נָגוּר	יָגוּר	תָּגוּר	אָגוּר	לָגוּר	to live
נָקוּם	יָקוּם	תָּקוּם	אָקוּם	לָקוּם	to get up
נָרוּץ	יָרוּץ	תָּרוּץ	אָרוּץ	לָרוּץ	to run
נָטוּס	יָטוּס	תָּטוּס	אָטוּס	לָטוּס	to fly
נָבוֹא	יָבוֹא	תָּבוֹא	אָבוֹא	לָבוֹא	to come
נָשִׁיר	יָשִׁיר	תָּשִׁיר	אָשִׁיר	לָשִׁיר	to sing
נָשִׂים	יָשִׂים	תָּשִׂים	אָשִׂים	לָשִׂים	to put

Binyan Pa'al, Group 2

And now, pronouns which require a suffix as well:

שם הפועל באנגלית	שֵׁם פֹּעַל Infinitive	את	אתם	הם
to live	לָגוּר	תָּגוּרִי	תָּגוּרוּ	יָגוּרוּ
to get up	לָקוּם	תָּקוּמִי	תָּקוּמוּ	יָקוּמוּ
to run	לָרוּץ	תָּרוּצִי	תָּרוּצוּ	יָרוּצוּ
to fly	לָטוּס	תָּטוּסִי	תָּטוּסוּ	יָטוּסוּ
to come	לָבוֹא	תָּבוֹאִי	תָּבוֹאוּ	יָבוֹאוּ
to sing	לָשִׁיר	תָּשִׁירִי	תָּשִׁירוּ	יָשִׁירוּ
to put	לָשִׂים	תָּשִׂימִי	תָּשִׂימוּ	יָשִׂימוּ

Binyan Pa'al, Group 2

סִפּוּר: לָטוּס לַיָּרֵחַ

אוֹצַר מִלִּים

moon	יָרֵחַ
boring	מְשַׁעֲמֵם
space	חָלָל
spaceship	חֲלָלִית
to fly off	לָעוּף
to fight	לָרִיב
condition	תְּנַאי
on one condition	בִּתְנַאי אֶחָד
very well	בְּסֵדֶר גָּמוּר

3. Practice future tense using a dialogue

Binyan Pa'al, Group 2

סיפור: לטוס לירח

גל: אבא...

אבא: כן.

גל: אני רוצה להיות אסטרונאוט. אני רוצה לטוס לירח.

אבא: אולי **תטוס** לאמריקה? זה יותר קרוב.

גל: אולי **אטוס** גם לאמריקה, אבל בטוח **אטוס** לירח.

אבא: אבל משעמם על הירח. אין שם אנשים.

גל: עכשיו אין שם אנשים, אבל אולי בעוד 10 שנים, אנשים **יגורו** על הירח.

אבא: מי **יגור** על הירח?

גל: הרבה אנשים - אסטרונאוטים ואסטרונומים... ואולי גם אני **אגור** שם.

אבא: לא, אל **תגור** על הירח! הירח רחוק מאבא ואמא.

גל: נו, מה הבעיה? **תבואו** לבקר.

אבא: איך **נבוא**?

גל: מה הבעיה? **תטוסו** בחללית. **תבואו** לבקר אותי כל חודש, ותביאו לי הרבה מתנות.

אבא: איפה **תשים** את המתנות?

גל: מה הבעיה? **אשים** אותן בבית שלי, על הירח.

אבא: אבל על הירח אין גרביטציה. המתנות **יעופו** לחלל.

גל: אה, נכון... טוב. אז אולי תביאו לי שוקולד. אני יכול לאכול את השוקולד מהר, לפני שהוא **יעוף** לחלל. זאת לא בעיה.

אבא: אהה. אני מבין. זאת לא בעיה לבוא לבקר בירח, זאת לא בעיה להביא מתנות... אבל יש עוד בעיה אחת - עם מי **תריב** על הירח?

גל: עם מי **אריב**? אני לא מבין.

אבא: כאן, בישראל, אתה רב עם האחים שלך ולפעמים עם החברים. האחים והחברים שלך **יגורו** בישראל, אבל אתה **תגור** לבד, על הירח... איך **תריבו**?

גל: אני לא יודע איך **נריב**! זאת באמת בעיה.

אבא: אז אולי לא **תגור** על הירח? אולי רק **תטוס** לבקר שם?

גל: אתה יודע מה? בסדר. לא **אגור** על הירח, אבל בתנאי אחד.

אבא: כן.

גל: **תשיר** לי שיר על הירח?

אבא: בסדר גמור, **אשיר.**

(אבא שר ומזייף: "חם על הירח"/ "לילה לילה מסתכלת הלבנה").

גל: אממ... אבא? אל **תשיר**. אני לא **אטוס**, באמת, רק אל **תשיר**.

Binyan Pa'al, Group 2

Now listen and read and check your comprehension sentence by sentence:

Gal: Dad…	גל: אבא...
Dad: Yes.	אבא: כן.
Gal: I want to be an astronaut. I want to fly to the moon.	גל: אני רוצה להיות אסטרונאוט. אני רוצה לטוס לירח.
Dad: Maybe you'll fly to America? It's closer.	אבא: אולי **תָטוּס** לאמריקה? זה יותר קרוב.
Gal: Maybe I'll fly to America too, but I'll surely fly to the moon.	גל: אולי **אָטוּס** גם לאמריקה, אבל בטוח **אָטוּס** לירח.
Dad: But it's boring on the moon. There are no people there.	אבא: אבל מְשַׁעֲמֵם על הירח. אין שם אנשים.
Gal: Now there are no people there, but maybe in 10 years, people will live on the moon.	גל: עכשיו אין שם אנשים, אבל אולי בעוד 10 שנים, אנשים **יָגוּרוּ** על הירח.
Dad: Who will live on the moon?	אבא: מי **יָגוּר** על הירח?
Gal: A lot of people - astronauts and astronomers… And maybe I'll live there too.	גל: הרבה אנשים - אסטרונאוטים ואסטרונומים... ואולי גם אני **אָגוּר** שם.
Dad: No, don't live on the moon! The moon is far from dad and mom.	אבא: לא, אל **תָגוּר** על הירח! הירח רחוק מאבא ואמא.
Gal: Well, what's the problem? You'll come [to] visit.	גל: נו, מה הבעיה? **תָבוֹאוּ** לבקר.
Dad: How will we come?	אבא: איך **נָבוֹא**?
Gal: What's the problem? You'll fly in a spaceship.	גל: מה הבעיה? **תָטוּסוּ** בחֲלָלִית.
You'll come visit me every month, and you'll bring me a lot of presents.	**תָבוֹאוּ** לבקר אותי כל חודש, ותביאו לי הרבה מתנות.
Dad: Where will you put the presents?	אבא: איפה **תָשִׂים** את המתנות?
Gal: What's the problem? I will put them in my house, on the moon.	גל: מה הבעיה? **אָשִׂים** אותן בבית שלי, על הירח.
Dad: But there's no gravitation on the moon. The gifts will fly off to space.	אבא: אבל על הירח אין גרביטציה. המתנות **יָעוּפוּ** לחָלָל.

Binyan Pa'al, Group 2

Gal: Oh, right… Okay. So maybe you'll bring me chocolate. I can eat the chocolate quickly, before it flies off to space. It's not a problem.	גל: אה, נכון... טוב. אז אולי תביאו לי שוקולד. אני יכול לאכול את השוקולד מהר, לפני שהוא **יָעוּף** לחָלָל. זאת לא בעיה.
Dad: Ahh, I understand. It's not a problem to come visit on the moon, it's not a problem to bring gifts… But there's one more problem - who will you fight with on the moon?	אבא: אהה, אני מבין. זאת לא בעיה לבוא לבקר בירח, זאת לא בעיה להביא מתנות... אבל יש עוד בעיה אחת - עם מי **תָרִיב** על הירח?
Gal: Who will I fight with? I don't understand.	גל: עם מי **אָרִיב?** אני לא מבין.
Dad: Here, in Israel, you fight with your brothers and sometimes with (your) friends. Your brothers and friends will live in Israel,	אבא: כאן, בישראל, אתה רב עם האחים שלך ולפעמים עם החברים. האחים והחברים שלך **יָגוּרוּ** בישראל,
but you'll live alone, on the moon… How will you fight?	אבל אתה **תָגוּר** לבד, על הירח... איך **תָרִיבוּ?**
Gal: I don't know how we'll fight! That's really a problem.	גל: אני לא יודע איך **נָרִיב!** זאת באמת בעיה.
Dad: So maybe you won't live on the moon?	אבא: אז אולי לא **תָגוּר** על הירח?
Maybe you'll just fly to visit there?	אולי רק **תָטוּס** לבקר שם?
Gal: You know what? Okay. I won't live on the moon, but on one condition.	גל: אתה יודע מה?! בסדר. לא **אָגוּר** על הירח, אבל בִּתְנַאי אחד.
Dad: Yes.	אבא: כן.
Gal: Will you sing me a song about the moon?	גל: **תָשִיר** לי שיר על הירח?
Dad: Very well, I will (sing).	אבא: בסדר גמור, **אָשִיר.**
(Dad sings off key)	(אבא שר ומזייף).
Gal: Ahm… dad? Don't sing.	גל: אממ... אבא? אל **תָשִיר.**
I won't fly, really, just don't sing.	אני לא **אָטוּס**, באמת, רק אל **תָשִיר.**

Binyan Pa'al, Group 2

Check yourself

1. Tell the story in Hebrew while reading the English text.
2. Fill in the right column in Hebrew and check yourself using the text on the previous page.

Gal: Dad…	
Dad: Yes.	
Gal: I want to be an astronaut. I want to fly to the moon.	
Dad: Maybe you'll fly to America? It's closer.	
Gal: Maybe I'll fly to America too, but I'll surely fly to the moon.	
Dad: But it's boring on the moon. There are no people there.	
Gal: Now there are no people there, but maybe in 10 years, people will live on the moon.	
Dad: Who will live on the moon?	
Gal: A lot of people - astronauts and astronomers…And maybe I'll live there too.	
Dad: No, don't live on the moon! The moon is far from dad and mom.	
Gal: Well, what's the problem? You'll come [to] visit.	
Dad: How will we come?	
Gal: What's the problem? You'll fly in a spaceship.	
You'll come visit me every month, and you'll bring me a lot of presents.	
Dad: Where will you put the presents?	

Binyan Pa'al, Group 2

Gal: What's the problem? I will put them in my house, on the moon.	
Dad: But there's no gravitation on the moon. The gifts will fly off to space.	
Gal: Oh, right… Okay. So maybe you'll bring me chocolate. I can eat the chocolate quickly, before it flies off to space. It's not a problem.	
Dad: Ahh, I understand. It's not a problem to come visit on the moon, it's not a problem to bring gifts… But there's one more problem - who will you fight with on the moon?	
Gal: Who will I fight with? I don't understand.	
Dad: Here, in Israel, you fight with your brothers and sometimes with (your) friends. Your brothers and friends will live in Israel,	
but you'll live alone, on the moon… How will you fight?	
Gal: I don't know how we'll fight! That's really a problem.	
Dad: So maybe you won't live on the moon?	
Maybe you'll just fly to visit there?	
Gal: You know what? Okay. I won't live on the moon, but on one condition.	
Dad: Yes.	
Gal: Will you sing me a song about the moon?	
Dad: Very well. I will (sing).	
(Dad sings off key)	
Gal: Ahm… dad? Don't sing.	
I won't fly, really, just don't sing.	

Binyan Pa'al, Group 2

Your Story – Binyan Pa'al 2

4. Create your own story

Now create your own story in Hebrew using the above story as an example.

Use all or part of the following verbs in future tense:

live; get up; run; fly; come; sing; put; fight

Binyan Pa'al, Group 2

בניין פעל, קבוצה 2

Vocabulary Test

5. Take a vocabulary test

Complete the chart according to the example:

הם	את	אתה/היא	אני	שֵׁם פֹּעַל Infinitive	שם הפועל באנגלית
יגורו	**תגורי**	**תגור**	**אגור**	**לָגוּר**	to live
					to get up
					to run
					to fly
					to come
					to sing
					to put

Exercising Binyan Pa'al 2

Listen to the following questions. Then write the questions from English to Hebrew. Check yourself by listening to the audio again.

Questions	Hebrew Translation
1. In a hundred years, will people live on the moon?	
2. At what time [hour] will you get up tomorrow morning?	
3. A lot of people will run in the Jerusalem Marathon. Will you run too?	
4. Will you and your friends fly? Where to?	
5. We want a lot of people to come to Israel. What can one do for it?	
6. If the Beatles [will] sing again, how many people will come to the concert?	
7. Where will you put all of the Ulpan books?	

Binyan Pa'al, Group 2

Write your answers in Hebrew here:

1.
2.
3.
4.
5.
6.
7.

Binyan Pa'al, Group 2

Exercise: Fill in the missing parts in the chart. (You don't have to know the meaning of the verbs). Check yourself by listening to the CD.

Conjugation	Infinitive	Pronoun
תזונו	לזון	אַתֶּם
צף	לצוף	הוּא
נצום	לצום	אֲנַחְנוּ
תדור	לדור	אַתָּה
תנועי	לנוע	אַתְּ
תתור	לתור	הִיא
יחושו	לחוש	הֵם
אצוץ	לצוץ	אֲנִי

Binyan Pa'al, Group 2

Imperative Form of Binyan Pa'al, Group 2

Let's use the future tense structure to create imperative form.

Remember: to create negative sentences the equivalent of **"Don't"** is אַל

Following are some examples of sentences using the imperative form:

Sing (m. sg.) an Israeli song for me, please.	תָּשִׁיר לִי שִׁיר יִשְׂרָאֵלִי, בְּבַקָּשָׁה.
Don't put (pl. m.) it here!	אַל תָּשִׂימוּ אֶת זֶה כָּאן!

Exercise: Write your own sentences in English using verbs from Binyan Pa'al, group 2 in imperative form. Use both, negative and positive structures. Translate those to Hebrew in the table below:

English	Hebrew

Binyan Pa'al, Group 2

Summary of Binyan Pa'al 2
Present and Future Tense

Notice how the basic sound of the Binyan remains the same, as only the suffixes and prefixes alternate.

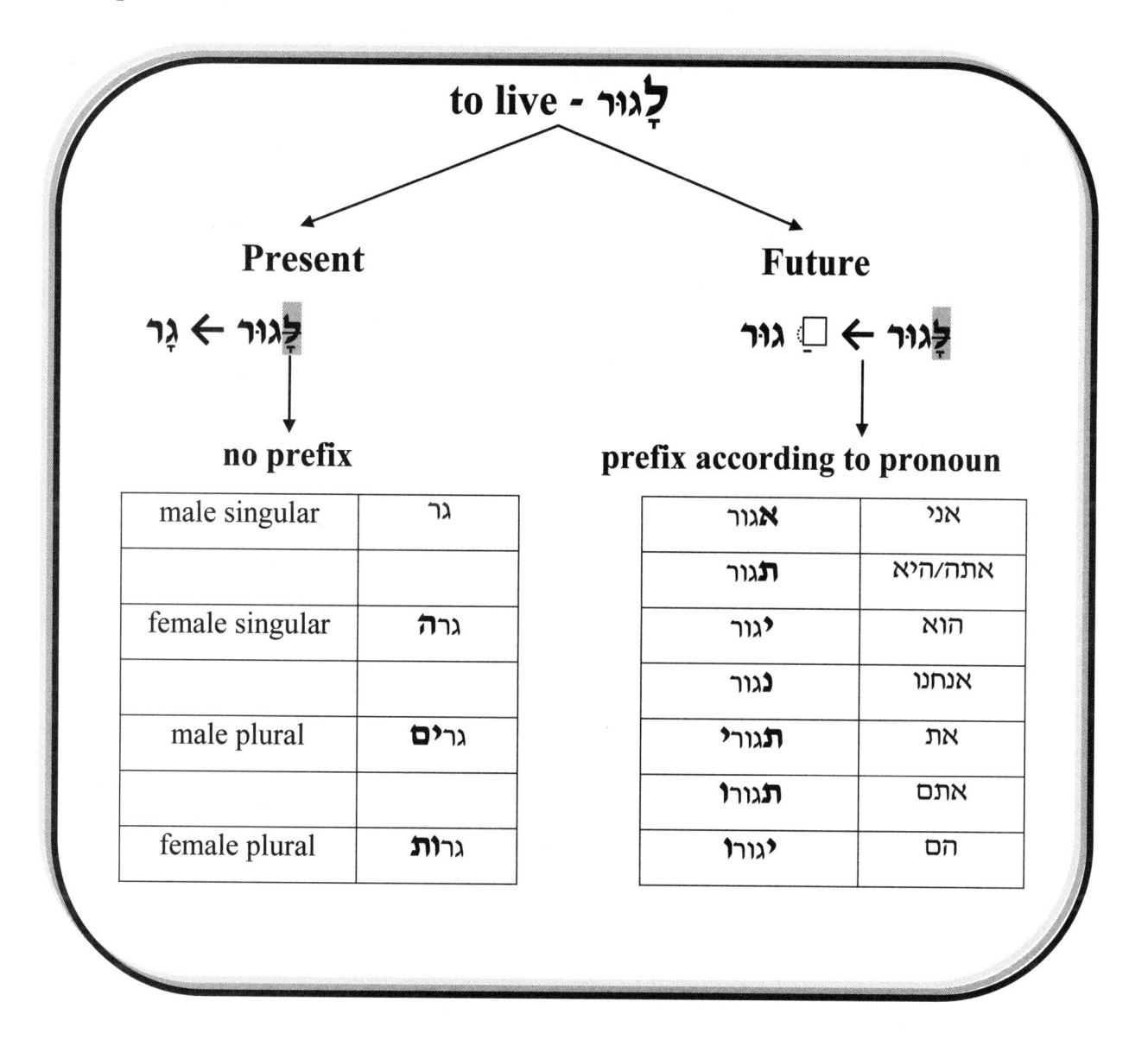

לָגוּר - to live

Present

גָר ← לָגוּר

no prefix

male singular	גר
female singular	גר**ה**
male plural	גר**ים**
female plural	גר**ות**

Future

גור ☐ ← לָגוּר

prefix according to pronoun

אני	**א**גור
אתה/היא	**ת**גור
הוא	**י**גור
אנחנו	**נ**גור
את	**ת**גור**י**
אתם	**ת**גור**ו**
הם	**י**גור**ו**

Binyan Pa'al, Group 3

בניין פעל, קבוצה 3

Infinitive form of each Binyan is the key to understanding the future tense structure. Let's review it now.

Infinitive Form

The infinitive form of Binyan Pa'al 3, has the following sound pattern:

LEE...OT

*(EE)...O... are the core sound pattern vowels

Example:

to buy - לִקְנוֹת

* The first vowel (EE) is in parenthesis because it's part of the prefix sound

Reminder of the infinitive form of the Binyan

Binyan Pa'al, Group 3

בניין פעל, קבוצה 3

Moving from Infinitive Form to Future Tense

1. Learn the structure of the Binyan in future tense

In Pa'al 3 we omit the infinitive form prefix **לְ**

The ending **וֹת** becomes **הֶ**, creating the sound pattern of:

...EE...EH

Instead of the **לְ** we use prefixes corresponding to the pronouns.

Suffixes will replace the **הֶ** sound. As an example let's use the verb to buy – **לִקְנוֹת**. Follow the arrows to find the prefixes used for each pronoun.

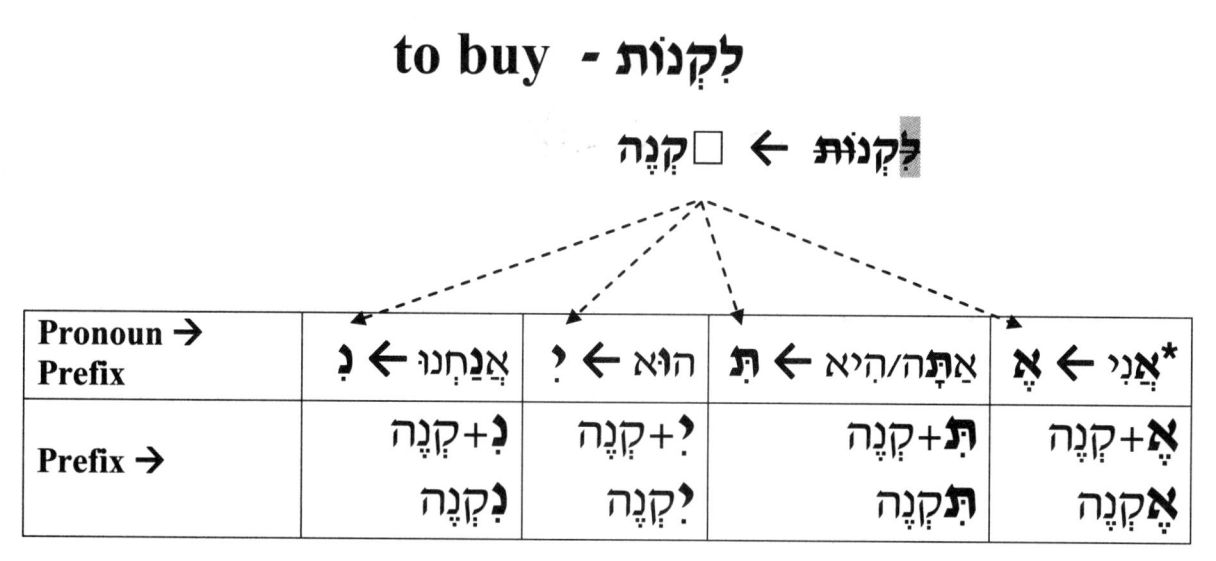

לִקְנוֹת - to buy

לִקְנוֹת ← □ קְנֶה

Pronoun → Prefix	אֲנִי* ← אֶ	אַתָּה/הִיא ← תִּ	הוּא ← יִ	אֲנַחְנוּ ← נִ
Prefix →	אֶ+קְנֶה אֶקְנֶה	תִּ+קְנֶה תִּקְנֶה	יִ+קְנֶה יִקְנֶה	נִ+קְנֶה נִקְנֶה

Now we will also need to add the corresponding suffixes:

Pronoun → Prefix & Suffix →	אַתְּ ← תִּ+י	אַתֶּם ← תִּ+וּ	הֵם ← יִ+וּ
Prefix & Suffix →	תִּ+קְנ+י תִּקְנִי	תִּ+קְנ+וּ תִּקְנוּ	יִ+קְנ+וּ יִקְנוּ

*Note that the music for **אֲנִי** is "E...EH"

בניין פעל, קבוצה 3

Moving from Infinitive Form to Future Tense

Starting with pronouns requiring only a prefix:

אנחנו	הוא	אתה/היא	אני	שֵׁם פֹּעַל Infinitive	שם הפועל באנגלית
נִשְׁתֶּה	יִשְׁתֶּה	תִּשְׁתֶּה	אֶשְׁתֶּה	לִשְׁתּוֹת	to drink
נִקְנֶה	יִקְנֶה	תִּקְנֶה	אֶקְנֶה	לִקְנוֹת	to buy
נִבְנֶה	יִבְנֶה	תִּבְנֶה	אֶבְנֶה	לִבְנוֹת	to build
נִבְכֶּה	יִבְכֶּה	תִּבְכֶּה	אֶבְכֶּה	לִבְכּוֹת	to cry
נִרְאֶה	יִרְאֶה	תִּרְאֶה	אֶרְאֶה	לִרְאוֹת	to see, to look
נַעֲשֶׂה	יַעֲשֶׂה	תַּעֲשֶׂה	אֶעֱשֶׂה	לַעֲשׂוֹת	to do

Binyan Pa'al, Group 3

Moving from Infinitive Form to Future Tense (Cont.)

אנחנו	הוא	אתה/היא	אני	שֵׁם פֹּעַל Infinitive	שם הפועל באנגלית
נַעֲנֶה	יַעֲנֶה	תַּעֲנֶה / תַּעֲנִי	אֶעֱנֶה / אֶעֱנֶה	לַעֲנוֹת	to answer
נִהְיֶה	יִהְיֶה	תִּהְיֶה	אֶהְיֶה	לִהְיוֹת	to be
נַעֲלֶה	יַעֲלֶה	תַּעֲלֶה / תַּעֲלִי	אֶעֱלֶה / אֶעֱלֶה	לַעֲלוֹת	to go up, to immigrate to Israel

And now, pronouns which require a suffix as well:

הם	אתם	את	שֵׁם פֹּעַל Infinitive	שם הפועל באנגלית
יִשְׁתּוּ	תִּשְׁתּוּ	תִּשְׁתִּי	לִשְׁתּוֹת	to drink
יִקְנוּ	תִּקְנוּ	תִּקְנִי	לִקְנוֹת	to buy
יִבְנוּ	תִּבְנוּ	תִּבְנִי	לִבְנוֹת	to build

Binyan Pa'al, Group 3

Moving from Infinitive Form to Future Tense (Cont.)

הם	אתם	את	שֵׁם פֹּעַל Infinitive	שם הפועל באנגלית
יִבְכּוּ	תִּבְכּוּ	תִּבְכִּי	לִבְכּוֹת	to cry
יִרְאוּ	תִּרְאוּ	תִּרְאִי	לִרְאוֹת	to see, to look
יַעֲשׂוּ	תַּעֲשׂוּ	תַּעֲשִׂי / תַּעֲשׂ	לַעֲשׂוֹת	to do
יַעֲנוּ	תַּעֲנוּ	תַּעֲנִי	לַעֲנוֹת	to answer
יִהְיוּ	תִּהְיוּ	תִּהְיִי	*לִהְיוֹת	*to be
יַעֲלוּ	תַּעֲלוּ	תַּעֲלִי	לַעֲלוֹת	to go up, to immigrate to Israel

*Please see special section related to the verb **לִהְיוֹת** on the next page.

Using the verb "to be" – לִהְיוֹת in the Future Tense

As mentioned earlier, the verb לִהְיוֹת = **to be**, is not used in Hebrew in the present tense. This verb has 4 main usages:

1. Location

In this case the verb לִהְיוֹת is conjugated according to the object / subject / person.

Present	Future	עָתִיד	הֹוֶה
I am home.	I will be home tomorrow.	אֶהְיֶה בַּבַּיִת מָחָר.	אֲנִי בַּבַּיִת.
They are in the cinema.	They will be in the cinema.	הֵם יִהְיוּ בַּקוֹלְנוֹעַ.	הֵם בַּקוֹלְנוֹעַ.
She is in the office.	She will be in the office.	הִיא תִּהְיֶה בַּמִּשְׂרָד.	הִיא בַּמִּשְׂרָד.

Exercise: Use the correct form of the verb לִהְיוֹת in the following sentences:

Example:

_____ מָחָר בַּבַּיִת?   לֹא. מָחָר _____ בָּעֲבוֹדָה.

תִּהְיֶה מָחָר בַּבַּיִת?   לֹא. מָחָר **אֶהְיֶה** בָּעֲבוֹדָה.

גַּם אַתֶּם לֹא __תִּהְיוּ__ בִּירוּשָׁלַיִם בְּשַׁבָּת?
לֹא, אֲנַחְנוּ __נִהְיֶה__ בְּטִיּוּל בַּגּוֹלָן.

שִׁמְעוֹן, אַתָּה __תִּהְיֶה__ בַּקַּיִץ בַּגּוֹלָן?
לֹא. __אֶהְיֶה__ בַּקַּיִץ בַּגָּלִיל.

הַיְלָדִים __יִהְיוּ__ בְּאֵילַת?
לֹא. הֵם __יִהְיוּ__ רַק בְּתֵל אָבִיב.

רֹאשׁ הַמֶּמְשָׁלָה __יִהְיֶה__ בְּבִקּוּר בְּאָמֶרִיקָה?
לֹא. הוּא __יִהְיֶה__ בָּאָרֶץ. אֲבָל כָּל הַמִּשְׁפָּחָה שֶׁלּוֹ __תִּהְיֶה__ בְּנְיוּ-יוֹרְק.

חַנָּה, __תִּהְיִי__ בַּבַּיִת מָחָר בָּעֶרֶב?
לֹא, __אֶהְיֶה__ בִּמְסִבָּה.

Binyan Pa'al, Group 3

Questions:

Write your full answers in Hebrew in this column	שאלות
	אֵיפֹה **תִּהְיֶה** מָחָר בָּעֶרֶב?
	מִי **יִהְיֶה** בְּשַׁבָּת בַּבַּיִת שֶׁלְּךָ?
	תִּהְיֶה פַּעַם (ever) בַּגָּלִיל?
	מִי **יִהְיֶה** הַנָּשִׂיא הַבָּא (next) שֶׁל יִשְׂרָאֵל?
	*הַמִּשְׁפָּחָה שֶׁלְּךָ **תִּהְיֶה** בָּאָרֶץ? *Note: מִשְׁפָּחָה in Hebrew is feminine.

CD3 Track 29

2. Condition / Situation

In this case the verb **לִהְיוֹת** is conjugated according to the object / person.

Present	Future	עָתִיד	הֹוֶה
You are manager.	You will be a manager.	**תִּהְיֶה** מְנַהֵל.	אַתָּה מְנַהֵל.
He is a tourist.	He will be a tourist.	הוּא **יִהְיֶה** תַּיָּר.	הוּא תַּיָּר.
We are hungry.	We will be hungry.	**נִהְיֶה** רְעֵבִים.	אֲנַחְנוּ רְעֵבִים.

Binyan Pa'al, Group 3

3. **Presence -** "There is" = יֵשׁ

In this case the verb **לִהְיוֹת** is conjugated according to the object / person.

Singular

Present	Future	עָתִיד	הֹוֶה
There is a window in the room.	There will be a window in the room.	יִהְיֶה חַלּוֹן בַּחֶדֶר.	יֵשׁ חַלּוֹן בַּחֶדֶר.
There is a party at home.	There will be a party at home.	**תִּהְיֶה** מְסִבָּה בַּבַּיִת.	יש מְסִבָּה בַּבַּיִת.

Plural

Present	Future	עָתִיד	הֹוֶה
There are good people at work.	There will be good people at work.	יִהְיוּ אֲנָשִׁים טוֹבִים בָּעֲבוֹדָה.	יֵשׁ אֲנָשִׁים טוֹבִים בָּעֲבוֹדָה.
There are nice pictures in the album.	There will be nice pictures in the album.	יִהְיוּ תְּמוּנוֹת יָפוֹת בָּאַלְבּוֹם.	יֵשׁ תְּמוּנוֹת יָפוֹת בָּאַלְבּוֹם.

Questions:

Write your full answers in Hebrew in this column	שאלות
	מִי **יִהְיֶה** הַנָּשִׂיא הַבָּא (next) שֶׁל אָמֶרִיקָה?
	תִּהְיֶה פַּעַם (ever) מְנַהֵל?
	הַמּוֹכְרִים בַּחֲנוּת **יִהְיוּ** נֶחְמָדִים?
	בַּחֹדֶשׁ הַבָּא **יִהְיוּ** הַרְבֵּה תַּיָּרִים בְּיִשְׂרָאֵל?
	בַּשָּׁנָה הַבָּאָה **יִהְיוּ** הַרְבֵּה עוֹלִים מֵרוּסְיָה?

Binyan Pa'al, Group 3

יֵשׁ / אֵין (בֶּעָתִיד)

מָחָר (future)	הַיּוֹם (present)
מָחָר יִהְיֶה בָּלָגָן.	הַיּוֹם יֵשׁ בָּלָגָן (mess).
מָחָר **תִּהְיֶה** מְסִבָּה.	הַיּוֹם יֵשׁ מְסִבָּה.
מָחָר יִהְיוּ הַרְבֵּה תַּיָּרִים בַּכֹּתֶל.	הַיּוֹם יֵשׁ הַרְבֵּה תַּיָּרִים בַּכֹּתֶל.
מָחָר **לֹא** יִהְיֶה בָּלָגָן.	הַיּוֹם אֵין בָּלָגָן (mess).
מָחָר לֹא **תִּהְיֶה** מְסִבָּה.	הַיּוֹם אֵין מְסִבָּה.
מָחָר לֹא יִהְיוּ הַרְבֵּה תַּיָּרִים בַּכֹּתֶל.	הַיּוֹם אֵין הַרְבֵּה תַּיָּרִים בַּכֹּתֶל.

Exercise: write the following sentences in the future tense.

מָחָר (future)	הַיּוֹם (present)
	בְּבֵית הַסֵּפֶר יֵשׁ מוֹרִים נֶחְמָדִים.
	בַּחֲנוּיוֹת יֵשׁ מוֹכְרוֹת נֶחְמָדוֹת.
	בַּמְּסִבָּה יֵשׁ מוּזִיקָה נְעִימָה.
	בַּמַּכֹּלֶת יֵשׁ לֶחֶם טָרִי.
	בַּקּוֹלְנוֹעַ אֵין כַּרְטִיסִים.
	בַּמִּסְעָדָה אֵין שְׁתִיָּה חֲרִיפָה.
	בְּסִינְגָּפּוּר אֵין לִכְלוּךְ.

4. Possession

This usage is usually a confusing one for English speakers. In English we have a special verb "to have" to describe possession of something.

In Hebrew we do not have a verb, but we use an expression יֵשׁ ל...

Present tense:

I have an apple.	יֵשׁ **לִי** תַּפּוּחַ.
He has an apple.	יֵשׁ **לוֹ** תַּפּוּחַ.
We have an apple.	יֵשׁ **לָנוּ** תַּפּוּחַ.
She has apples.	יֵשׁ **לָהּ** תַּפּוּחִים.

Binyan Pa'al, Group 3

Future tense:

The verb **להיות** is used according to the subject and **not** according to the owner of the subject in one of the following forms:

יִהְיוּ   תִּהְיֶה   יִהְיֶה

Examples:

I will have an apple. → יִהְיֶה לִי תַּפּוּחַ. (The word **תַּפּוּחַ** is single, thus **יִהְיֶה**)

He will have an apple. → יִהְיֶה לוֹ תַּפּוּחַ. (The word **תַּפּוּחַ** is single, thus **יִהְיֶה**)

We will have an apple. → יִהְיֶה לָנוּ תַּפּוּחַ. (The word **תַּפּוּחַ** is single, thus **יִהְיֶה**)

She will have apples (plural). → יִהְיוּ לָהּ תַּפּוּחִים. (The word **תַּפּוּחִים** is plural, thus **יִהְיוּ**)

*Note: In the future tense the verb **להיות** is used either in the single or the plural, masculine or feminine form according to the related subject*

Present	Future	עָתִיד	הֹוֶה
I have a nice house.	I will have a nice house.	יִהְיֶה לִי בַּיִת יָפֶה.	יֵשׁ לִי בַּיִת יָפֶה.
I have a nice job.	I will have a nice job.	תִּהְיֶה לִי עֲבוֹדָה טוֹבָה.	יֵשׁ לִי עֲבוֹדָה טוֹבָה.
I have a lot of friends.	I will have a lot of friends.	יִהְיוּ לִי הַרְבֵּה חֲבֵרִים.	יֵשׁ לִי הַרְבֵּה חֲבֵרִים.

Binyan Pa'al, Group 3

Possession - additional examples:

1. Masculine subject

Present	Future	עָתִיד	הֹוֶה
I have a house.	I will have a house.	יִהְיֶה לִי בַּיִת.	יֵשׁ לִי בַּיִת.
You have a house.	You will have a house.	יִהְיֶה לְךָ בַּיִת.	יֵשׁ לְךָ בַּיִת.
They have a house.	They will have a house.	יִהְיֶה לָהֶם בַּיִת.	יֵשׁ לָהֶם בַּיִת.
You (pl.) have a house.	You will have a house.	יִהְיֶה לָכֶם בַּיִת.	יֵשׁ לָכֶם בַּיִת.

2. Feminine subject

Present	Future	עָתִיד	הֹוֶה
I have a job.	I will have a job.	תִּהְיֶה לִי עֲבוֹדָה.	יֵשׁ לִי עֲבוֹדָה.
You have a job.	You will have a job.	תִּהְיֶה לָכֶם עֲבוֹדָה.	יֵשׁ לָכֶם עֲבוֹדָה.
They have a job.	They will have a job.	תִּהְיֶה לָהֶם עֲבוֹדָה.	יֵשׁ לָהֶם עֲבוֹדָה.
We have a job.	We will have a job.	תִּהְיֶה לָנוּ עֲבוֹדָה.	יֵשׁ לָנוּ עֲבוֹדָה.

3. Plural subjects

Present	Future	עָתִיד	הֹוֶה
I have friends.	I will have friends.	יִהְיוּ לִי חֲבֵרִים.	יֵשׁ לִי חֲבֵרִים.
You have friends.	You will have friends.	יִהְיוּ לָכֶם חֲבֵרִים.	יֵשׁ לָכֶם חֲבֵרִים.
They have friends.	They will have friends.	יִהְיוּ לָהֶם חֲבֵרִים.	יֵשׁ לָהֶם חֲבֵרִים.
We have friends.	We will have friends.	יִהְיוּ לָנוּ חֲבֵרִים.	יֵשׁ לָנוּ חֲבֵרִים.

Binyan Pa'al, Group 3

יֵשׁ לִי / אֵין לִי (עתיד) I have / I don't have

מָחָר (future)	הַיּוֹם (present)
יִהְיֶה לִי כֶּלֶב.	יֵשׁ לִי כֶּלֶב.
תִּהְיֶה לָנוּ דִּירָה.	יֵשׁ לָנוּ דִּירָה.
יִהְיוּ לָכֶם חֲבֵרִים.	יֵשׁ לָכֶם חֲבֵרִים.
לֹא יִהְיֶה לִי כֶּלֶב.	אֵין לִי כֶּלֶב.
לֹא תִּהְיֶה לָנוּ דִּירָה.	אֵין לָנוּ דִּירָה.
לֹא יִהְיוּ לָכֶם חֲבֵרִים.	אֵין לָכֶם חֲבֵרִים.

Exercise: Write the following questions first in present, then in the future tense.

עָתִיד	הֹוֶה
	יֵשׁ לְךָ זְמַן?
	יֵשׁ לְךָ עֲבוֹדָה?
	יֵשׁ לְיִשְׂרָאֵל* הַרְבֵּה חֲבֵרִים בָּעוֹלָם?
	יֵשׁ לָכֶם תָּכְנִיּוֹת?
	יֵשׁ לָהֶם יְלָדִים?
	יֵשׁ לָהּ סְפָרִים?
	יֵשׁ לְךָ דִּירָה בִּירוּשָׁלַיִם?
	כַּמָּה עוֹבְדִים יֵשׁ לְךָ?

*Country and city names in Hebrew are feminine.

Binyan Pa'al, Group 3

סִפּוּר: קְנִיּוֹת עִם אִמָּא

אוֹצַר מִלִּים

mall	קַנְיוֹן
gift	מַתָּנָה
cinema	קוֹלְנוֹעַ
vacation	חוּפְשָׁה
thirsty	צָמֵא
a nag	נוּדְנִיק
favor	טוֹבָה

3. Practice future tense using a dialogue

סיפור: קניות עם אמא

אמא: גדי, אני הולכת לקניון. אתה רוצה לבוא איתי?
גדי: לקניון? מה **נעשה** שם?
אמא: **נקנה** לאבא מתנה ליום ההולדת.
גדי: בסדר. אני בא.

***

גדי: אמא, אולי **נעלה** ל- TOYS'R'US ?
אמא: טויז אר אס? מה **נעשה** שם?
גדי: **נקנה** לי לגו.
אמא: לגו? מה **תעשה** בלגו?
גדי: אבא ואני **נבנה** דברים יפים יחד.
אמא: לא, אתם לא **תבנו** יחד. אבא **יבנה** הכל לבד, ואתה **תראה** טלוויזיה, נכון?
גדי: אז אולי **נקנה** לי...
אמא: גדי, עכשיו אנחנו קונים מתנה לאבא. בפברואר יש לך יום-הולדת, ואז כולם **יקנו** לך מתנות.
גדי: בסדר. הי, אמא, **תראי**, יש פה קולנוע. אולי **נראה** סרט?
אמא: לא, אין לנו זמן עכשיו. בחופשה **תראה** הרבה סרטים, בסדר?
גדי: טוב, נו... אמא, אני צמא. **תקני** לי משהו לשתות.
אמא: אתה צמא? **תשתה** מים. יש לך מים בתיק.
גדי: בסדר. אמא, אני רעב, **תקני** לי משהו לאכול.
אמא: גדי, האוכל בקניון ג'אנק. עוד מעט **נעלה** הביתה ותאכל ארוחה טובה.
גדי: טוב. אמא, אני עייף...
אמא: גדי, מספיק! אל **תהיה** נודניק. זאת הפעם האחרונה שאני נוסעת איתך לקניון.
גדי: את תמיד אומרת את זה.
אמא: הפעם זה באמת.
גדי: את תמיד אומרת: "הפעם זה באמת".
אמא: הפעם זה באמת, באמת. אתה **תראה** : בפעם הבאה שאלך לקניון, אתה תישאר בבית.
גדי: ואם **אבכה**? הנה, אני בוכה עכשיו... אההה...
אמא: נו, גדי, אל **תעשה** סצנה... טוב, **תהיה** ילד טוב ובבית **תראה** טלוויזיה.
גדי: עד 10 בלילה?
אמא: עד 10 בלילה. רק **תעשה** לי טובה, **תהיה** קצת בשקט.

Binyan Pa'al, Group 3

Now listen and read and check your comprehension sentence by sentence:

Mom: Gadi, I'm going to the mall. Do you want to come with me?	אמא : גדי, אני הולכת לקניון. אתה רוצה לבוא איתי?
Gadi: To the mall? What will we do there?	גדי : לקניון? מה **נַעֲשֶׂה** שם?
Mom: We'll buy dad a gift for (his) birthday.	אמא : **נִקְנֶה** לאבא מתנה ליום ההולדת.
Gadi: Okay, I'm coming. Mom, maybe we'll go up to Toys 'R Us?	גדי : בסדר. אני בא. אמא, אולי **נַעֲלֶה** ל- TOYS'R'US ?
Mom: Toys 'R Us? What will we do there?	אמא : טויז אר אס? מה **נַעֲשֶׂה** שם?
Gadi: We'll buy me Lego.	גדי : **נִקְנֶה** לי לגו.
Mom: Lego? What will you do with Lego?	אמא : לגו? מה **תַּעֲשֶׂה** בלגו?
Gadi: Dad and I will build beautiful things together.	גדי : אבא ואני **נִבְנֶה** דברים יפים יחד.
Mom: No, you won't build together. Dad will build everything alone, and you'll watch TV, right?	אמא : לא, אתם לא **תִּבְנוּ** יחד. אבא **יִבְנֶה** הכל לבד, ואתה **תִּרְאֶה** טלוויזיה, נכון?
Gadi: So maybe we'll buy me…	גדי : אז אולי **נִקְנֶה** לי...
Mom: Gadi, now we're buying a gift for dad. In February you have your birthday, and then everyone will buy you gifts.	אמא : גדי, עכשיו אנחנו קונים מתנה לאבא. בפברואר יש לך יום-הולדת, ואז כולם **יִקְנוּ** לך מתנות.
Gadi: Okay. Hey, mom, look, there's a cinema here. Maybe we'll see a movie?	גדי : בסדר. הי, אמא, **תִּרְאִי**, יש פה קולנוע. אולי **נִרְאֶה** סרט?
Mom: No, we don't have time now. On (your) vacation you'll see lots of movies, okay?	אמא : לא, אין לנו זמן עכשיו. בחופשה **תִּרְאֶה** הרבה סרטים, בסדר?
Gadi: Okay… Mom, I'm thirsty. Buy me something to drink.	גדי : טוב, נו... אמא, אני צמא. **תִּקְנִי** לי משהו לשתות.

Binyan Pa'al, Group 3

Mom: Are you thirsty? Drink water. You have water in your bag.	אמא : אתה צמא? **תִּשְׁתֶּה** מים. יש לך מים בתיק.
Gadi: Okay. Mom, I'm hungry, buy me something to eat.	גדי : בסדר. אמא, אני רעב, **תִּקְנִי** לי משהו לאכול.
Mom: Gadi, the food at the mall is junk. Soon we'll go [up] home and you'll eat a good meal.	אמא : גדי, האוכל בקניון ג'אנק. עוד מעט **נַעֲלֶה** הביתה ותֹאכַל ארוחה טובה.
Gadi: Okay. Mom, I'm tired…	גדי : טוב. אמא, אני עָיֵיף...
Mom: Gadi, enough! Don't be a nag. This is the last time I'm going to the mall with you.	אמא : גדי, מספיק! אל **תִּהְיֶה** נודניק. זאת הפעם האחרונה שאני נוסעת איתך לקניון.
Gadi: You always say that.	גדי : את תמיד אומרת את זה.
Mom: This time it's for real.	אמא : הפעם זה באמת.
Gadi: You always say "This time it's for real."	גדי : את תמיד אומרת: "הפעם זה באמת".
Mom: This time it's really for real. You'll see: the next time I'll go to the mall, you'll stay home.	אמא : הפעם זה באמת, באמת. אתה **תִּרְאֶה**: בפעם הבאה שאלך לקניון, אתה תישאר בבית.
Gadi: And if I (will) cry? Here, I'm crying now…	גדי : ואם **אֶבְכֶּה**? הנה, אני בוכה עכשיו...
Mom: Come on, Gadi, don't make a scene…	אמא : נו, גדי, אל **תַּעֲשֶׂה** סצנה...
Okay, you'll be a good boy,	טוב, **תִּהְיֶה** ילד טוב,
and at home you'll watch TV.	ובבית **תִּרְאֶה** טלוויזיה.
Gadi: Until 10 at night?	גדי : עד 10 בלילה?
Mom: Until 10 at night, just do me a favor,	אמא : עד 10 בלילה. רק **תַּעֲשֶׂה** לי טובה,
be quiet for a little while (lit. be a little quiet).	**תִּהְיֶה** קצת בשקט.

Binyan Pa'al, Group 3

Check yourself

1. Tell the dialogue in Hebrew while reading the English text.
2. Fill in the right column in Hebrew and check yourself using the text on the previous page.

Mom: Gadi, I'm going to the mall. Do you want to come with me?	
Gadi: To the mall? What will we do there?	
Mom: We'll buy dad a gift for (his) birthday.	
Gadi: Okay, I'm coming. Mom, maybe we'll go up to Toys 'R Us?	
Mom: Toys 'R Us? What will we do there?	
Gadi: We'll buy me Lego.	
Mom: Lego? What will you do with Lego?	
Gadi: Dad and I will build beautiful things together.	
Mom: No, you won't build together.	
Dad will build everything alone, and you'll watch TV, right?	
Gadi: So maybe we'll buy me…	
Mom: Gadi, now we're buying a gift for dad. In February you have your birthday, and then everyone will buy you gifts.	
Gadi: Okay. Hey, mom, look, there's a cinema here.	
Maybe we'll see a movie?	
Mom: No, we don't have time now. On (your) vacation you'll see lots of movies,	
Gadi: Okay… Mom, I'm thirsty. Buy me something to drink.	

Binyan Pa'al, Group 3

Mom: Are you thirsty? Drink water. You have water in your bag.	
Gadi: Okay. Mom, I'm hungry, buy me something to eat.	
Mom: Gadi, the food at the mall is junk. Soon we'll go [up] home and you'll eat a good meal.	
Gadi: Okay. Mom, I'm tired…	
Mom: Gadi, enough! Don't be a nag. This is the last time I'm going to the mall with you.	
Gadi: You always say that.	
Mom: This time it's for real.	
Gadi: You always say "This time it's for real."	
Mom: This time it's really for real. You'll see: the next time I'll go to the mall, you'll stay home.	
Gadi: And if I (will) cry? Here, I'm crying now…	
Mom: Come on, Gadi, don't make a scene…	
Okay, you'll be a good boy,	
and at home you'll watch TV.	
Gadi: Until 10 at night?	
Mom: Until 10 at night, just do me a favor,	
be quiet for a little while (lit. be a little quiet).	

Binyan Pa'al, Group 3

4. Create your own story

Your Story – Binyan Pa'al 3

Now create your own story in Hebrew using the above story as an example.

Use all or part of the following verbs in future tense:

do; answer; be; go up; see

Binyan Pa'al, Group 3

בניין פעל, קבוצה 3

Vocabulary Test

5. Take a vocabulary test

Complete the chart according to the example:

הם	את	אתה/היא	אני	שֵׁם פֹּעַל Infinitive	שם הפועל באנגלית
ישתו	תשתי	תשתה	אשתה	לִשְׁתּוֹת	to drink
					to buy
					to build
					to cry
					to see, to look
					to do

Binyan Pa'al, Group 3

Vocabulary Test (Cont.)

הם	את	אתה/היא	אני	שֵׁם פֹּעַל Infinitive	שם הפועל באנגלית
					to answer
					to be
					to go up, to immigrate to Israel

Exercising Binyan Pa'al 3 – Future Tense

Listen to the following questions. Then write the questions from English to Hebrew. Check yourself by listening to the audio again.

Questions	Hebrew Translation
1. What will you (m. sg.) drink in the morning?	
2. Will they be in Israel next year?	
3. Will you (f.) build a house in Israel?	
4. Will she answer the phone in Hebrew?	
5. Will you (m. pl.) buy a lot of things in Israel?	
6. Will the children cry at night?	

Binyan Pa'al, Group 3

Write your answers in Hebrew here:

1.

2.

3.

4.

5.

6.

Binyan Pa'al, Group 3

Exercise: Fill in the missing parts in the chart. (You don't have to know the meaning of the verbs). Check yourself by listening to the CD.

Conjugation	Infinitive	Pronoun
תִּקְלוּ	לקלות	אַתֶּם
וכפה	לכפות	הוּא
נצפה	לצפות	אֲנַחְנוּ
תצלה	לצלות	אַתָּה
תשהי	לשהות	אַתְּ
תבהה	לבהות	הִיא
יגבו	לגבות	הֵם
אזרה	לזרות	אֲנִי

Binyan Pa'al, Group 3

Imperative Form of Binyan Pa'al, Group 3

Let's use the future tense structure to create imperative form.

Remember: to create negative sentences the equivalent of **"Don't"** is אַל.

Following are some examples of sentences using the imperative form:

Answer (f. sg.) the phone quickly!	תַּעֲנִי לַטֶּלֶפוֹן מַהֵר!
Don't buy (m. sg.) cottage cheese in the supermarket. Buy milk.	אַל תִּקְנֶה גְּבִינַת קוֹטֶג' בַּסוּפֶּרְמַרְקֶט. תִּקְנֶה חָלָב.

Exercise: Write your own sentences in English using verbs from Binyan Pa'al, group 3 in imperative form. Use both, negative and positive structures. Translate those to Hebrew in the table below:

English	Hebrew

Summary of Binyan Pa'al 3
Present and Future Tense

Notice how the basic sound of the Binyan remains the same, as only the suffixes and prefixes alternate.

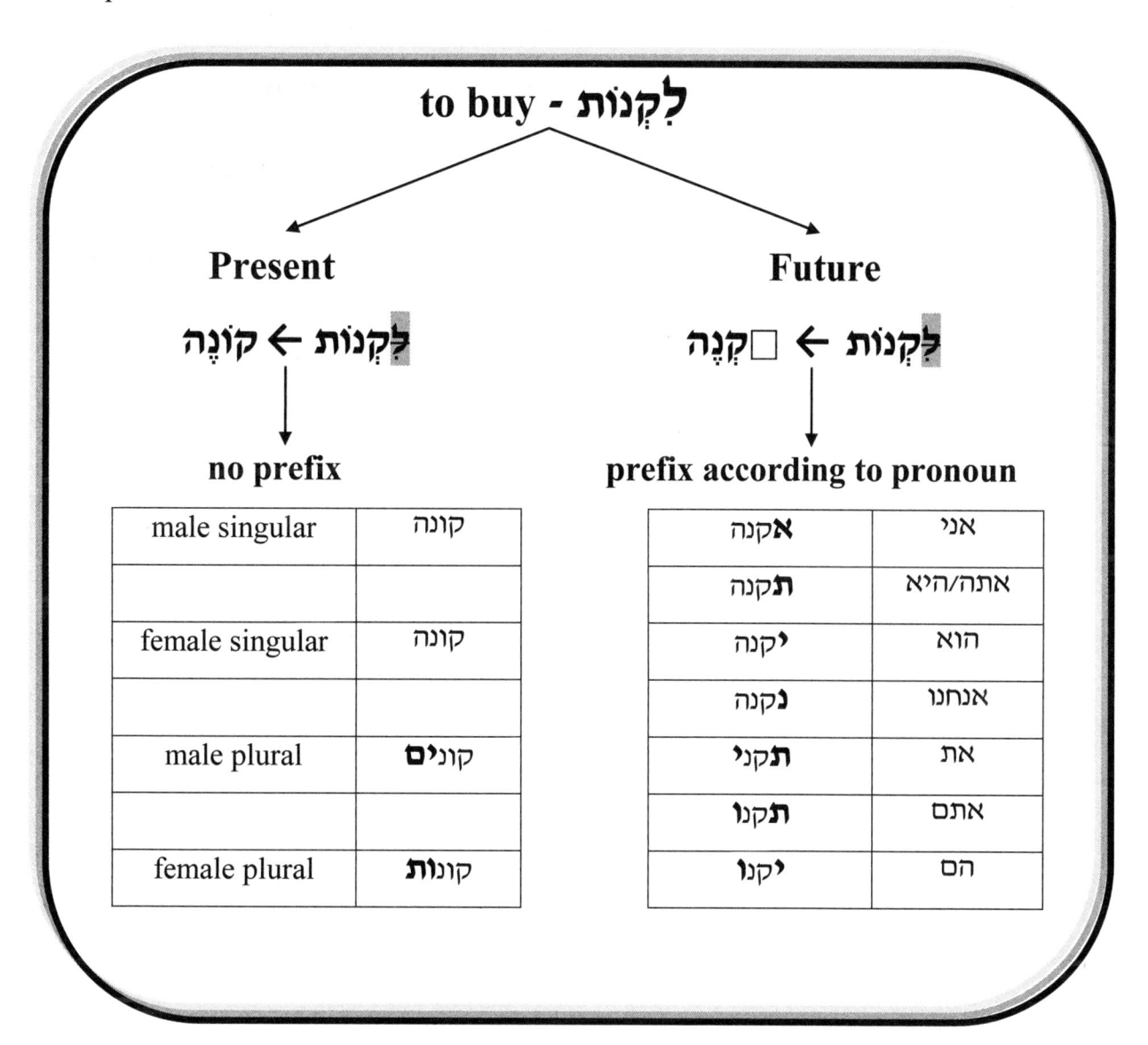

לִקְנוֹת - to buy

Present

קוֹנֶה ← לִקְנוֹת

no prefix

male singular	קונה
female singular	קונה
male plural	קונ**ים**
female plural	קונ**ות**

Future

קְנֶה☐ ← לִקְנוֹת

prefix according to pronoun

אני	**א**קנה
אתה/היא	**ת**קנה
הוא	**י**קנה
אנחנו	**נ**קנה
את	**ת**קנ**י**
אתם	**ת**קנ**ו**
הם	**י**קנ**ו**

Prepositions

מִלּוֹת יַחַס

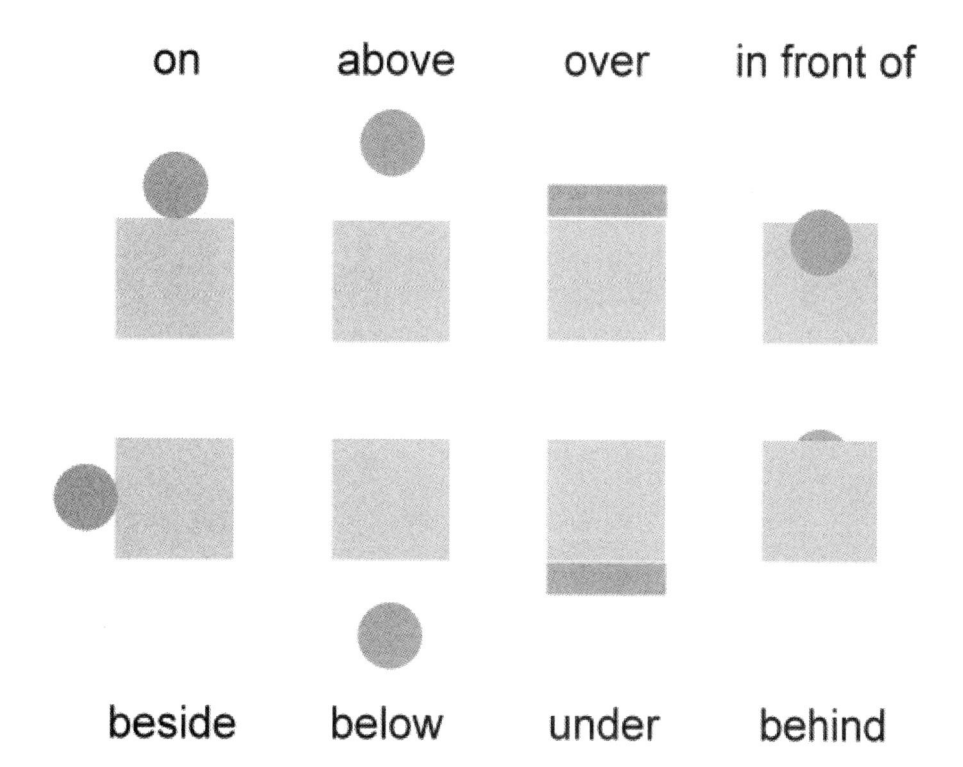

on	above	over	in front of
beside	below	under	behind

About Prepositions in Hebrew

In Hebrew, correct usage of prepositions is a major key in building sentences.

Prepositions usually come after a verb. The prepositions change according to the subject to which the verb refers.

Proper use of prepositions helps the sentence become perfect; improper use really spoils the sentence and may cause misunderstanding of the meaning one wants to convey.

On the following page you will find a chart with several common verbs and prepositions used with them.

You can also use this chart to populate it with new verbs you study and their respective prepositions

Prepositions

טבלת מילות יחס
Preposition Chart

Please translate the verbs into English and fill those in the respective locations in the chart. Continue populating this chart as you get to know additional verbs. In the following charts we will indicate the closest equivalent preposition in English, but please note that in each language the usage of prepositions is unique and it also changes in conjunction with different verbs,

from – מ		to – אל		to – ל		with - עם		את no English equivalent	
אנגלית	עברית	אנגלית	עברית	אנגלית	עברית	אנגלית	עברית	אנגלית	עברית
	להיפרד		לבוא		לבוא		להיפגש		לפגוש
	לקבל		לצלצל		לצלצל		לדבר		להכיר
	לקחת		להביא		להביא		לעבוד		להזמין
	להוציא		להתקשר		להתקשר				לבקר
	לבקש		לטלפן		לטלפן		לנסוע		לאהוב
			להגיע		להגיע		להתפלל		לשמוע
			לכתוב		לכתוב		לשתות		לראות
			להיכנס		להיכנס		ללמוד		להבין
			לשלוח		לשלוח				לחפש
					לספר				לקחת
					להפריע				לקרוא
					להיבחר				לאכול
					לעזור				
					להגיד				
					לומר				
					לתת				

Prepositions

Prepositions Track 3

טבלת מילות יחס

Please translate the verbs into English and fill those in the respective locations in the chart. Continue populating this chart as you get to know additional verbs

שֶ - that*		אחרי - after		לפני - before		ב - in		על – on, about	
אנגלית	עברית	אנגלית	עברית	אנגלית	עברית	אנגלית	עברית	אנגלית	עברית
	לרצות		לעמוד		לעמוד		להישאר		לחשוב
	לחשוב		לבוא		לבוא		להתקדם		לדבר
	להבין		לשבת		לשבת		לגור		להסתכל
	לראות						להיות		
	לשמוע						להשתמש		
	לומר								
	לבקש								

* Using the preposition שֶ in Hebrew is similar to using "**that**" in English.

For instance:

I think **that** Moshe is a good student – אני חושב שמשה הוא תלמיד טוב
I see **that** there are many people there – אני רואה שיש הרבה אנשי שם

However in certain cases the usage of שֶ is quite different from English.

When the meaning of a sentence calls for a certain action, the verb used with the preposition שֶ is conjugated in the future form.

For instance:

I want [that] you to [will] go home – אני רוצה שתלך הביתה

I am asking [that] you to [will] sit down – אני מבקש שתשב

Asking questions with prepositions

When you ask a question in Hebrew, the preposition "jumps" from its usual place to the beginning of the question.

For example:

Asking the question: "Who do you want to meet **with**"?

To meet **with** = עִם לְהִיפָּגֵשׁ

In English, the preposition jumps to the end of the question:

Example:

Who do you want to meet **with**?

Therefore a lot of times English speakers try to wrongly mimic it in Hebrew and put the preposition at the end of the question:

Wrong ➔ ?מִי אַתָּה רוֹצֶה לְהִיפָּגֵשׁ עִם

When asking a question in Hebrew, the preposition has to "jump" to the beginning of the question:

Right ➔ עִם מִי אַתָּה רוֹצֶה לְהִיפָּגֵשׁ? עִם

Practice asking questions with prepositions

Translate the following questions. Check yourself by listening to the CD.

- What do you want to talk about?
- Who do you want to talk to tonight?
- Who do you want to meet?
- Who do you want to visit?
- Who do you want to invite for dinner?
- Who do you want to see?
- Which countries do you want to visit?
- What are you looking for?
- What is he talking about?
- Who do you write an e-mail to?
- What do you think about?
- Who do you love?
- Where are you going to?
- Who are you calling today?
- What time do you get up?
- What are you looking for?
- What are you looking at?
- Who do you want to give this present to?
- What are you waiting for?

Combining preposition with a pronoun

Previously we saw the structure of combining a preposition with a pronoun. The structure is as shown in the second column of the following table.

In Hebrew, prepositions can be directly connected in writing to pronouns creating one combined word.

The endings of these combined words are the same for all prepositions corresponding to the pronouns.

This can be seen in the second column of the following charts.

	של		ל....	General structure	Pronoun
Mine	שֶׁלִי	(To) me	לִי	◻ִי	אֲנִי
Yours (m)	שֶׁלְךָ	(To) you	לְךָ	◻ְךָ	אַתָּה
Yours (f)	שֶׁלָךְ	(To) you	לָךְ	◻ָךְ	אַתְּ
His	שֶׁלוֹ	(To) him	לוֹ	◻וֹ	הוּא
Hers	שֶׁלָה	(To) her	לָה	◻ָה	הִיא
Ours	שֶׁלָנוּ	(To) us	לָנוּ	◻ָנוּ	אָנוּ
Yours (m)	שֶׁלָכֶם	(To) you (m, plural)	לָכֶם	◻ָכֶם	אַתֶּם
Yours (f)	שֶׁלָכֶן	(To) you (f, plural)	לָכֶן	◻ָכֶן	אַתֶּן *
Theirs (m)	שֶׁלָהֶם	(To) them (m, plural)	לָהֶם	◻ָהֶם	הֵם
Theirs (f)	שֶׁלָהֶן	(To) them (m, plural)	לָהֶן	◻ָהֶן	הֵן *

* Please note: The feminine forms of אַתֶּן / הֵן and respectively לָכֶן / לָהֶן are not in use in modern Hebrew. Usually people use שֶׁלָכֶם / שֶׁלָהֶם for both masculine and feminine.

Three prepositions that are combined with pronouns

from ...מ (when combined - turns into... ממ)	with – עם (when combined - turns into... אית)	the - אֶת (when combined- turns into... אוֹת)	General structure	Pronoun
from me מִמֶּנִי	with me אִתִּי	me אוֹתִי	◻ִי	אֲנִי
from you מִמְּךָ	with you אִתְּךָ	you אוֹתְךָ	◻ְךָ	אַתָּה
from you מִמֵּךְ	with you אִתָּךְ	you אוֹתָךְ	◻ָךְ	אַתְּ
from him מִמֶּנּוּ	with him אִתּוֹ	him אוֹתוֹ	◻וֹ	הוּא
from her מִמֶּנָּה	with her אִתָּהּ	her אוֹתָהּ	◻ָהּ	הִיא
from us מֵאִתָּנוּ (plural, m)	with us אִתָּנוּ	us אוֹתָנוּ	◻ָנוּ	אָנוּ
from you מִכֶּם (plural, m)	with you אִתְּכֶם (plural, m)	you (plural, m) אֶתְכֶם	◻ְכֶם	אַתֶּם
from you מִכֶּן (plural, f)	with you אִתְּכֶן (plural, f)	you (plural, f) אֶתְכֶן	◻ְכֶן	* אַתֶּן
from them (m) מֵהֶם	with them (m) אִתָּם	them (m) אוֹתָם	◻ְהֶם	הֵם
from them (f) מֵהֶן	with them (f) אִתָּן	them (f) אוֹתָן	◻ְהֶן	* הֵן

* Please note: The feminine forms of אַתֶּן / הֵן and respectively אֶתְכֶן / אוֹתָן etc. are not in use in modern Hebrew. Usually people use the masculine form of אוֹתָם / אֶתְכֶם etc. for both masculine and feminine.

Examples:

The - אֶת	אני רואה אותך - I see you, אתה מזמין אותה - You invite her
With - עִם	הוא מדבר איתה – He talks with her, הם לומדים איתי – They study with me
From - מ	מה אתה רוצה ממני? – What do you want from me?

Please note:

1) In modern Hebrew the preposition עם (with) when is combined with pronouns turns to את .
   For instance, in modern Hebrew we use אִתְּךָ (with you) instead of עִמְּךָ .

2) When preposition מ (from) is combined with pronouns, the first letter א of the pronoun in most cases turns to מ .
   For instance, instead of מֵאֲנִי (from me) - we say מִמֶּנִי .

Prepositions

Prepositions Track 8

תרגיל – הטיה של מילות יחס

Exercise: Conjugate the following prepositions according to the example.

אֵצֶל	עֲבוּר	בְּ..	בִּשְׁבִיל	בְּעֶצֶם	General structure	Pronoun
אֶצְלִי — At my place	עֲבוּרִי — For me	בִּי — In me	בִּשְׁבִילִי — For me	בְּעַצְמִי — By myself	◻ִי	אֲנִי
				בְּעַצְמְךָ	◻ְךָ	אַתָּה
				בְּעַצְמֵךְ	◻ֵךְ	אַתְּ
				בְּעַצְמוֹ	◻וֹ	הוּא
				בְּעַצְמָהּ	◻ָהּ	הִיא
				בְּעַצְמֵנוּ	◻ֵנוּ	אָנוּ
				בְּעַצְמְכֶם	◻ְכֶם	אַתֶּם
				בְּעַצְמָם	◻ָם	הֵם

* Please note that such conjugation is called נטייה ביחיד (singular form), and you can conjugate any noun in such a form if the noun appears in the singular form.

For instance:

יַלְדוּת (childhood)	מְדִינָה (country)*	תּוֹר (line, turn)	General structure	Pronoun
יַלְדוּתִי	מְדִינָתִי	תּוֹרִי - my turn	◻ִי	אֲנִי
יַלְדוּתְךָ	מְדִינָתְךָ	תּוֹרְךָ	◻ְךָ	אַתָּה
יַלְדוּתֵךְ	מְדִינָתֵךְ	תּוֹרֵךְ	◻ֵךְ	אַתְּ
יַלְדוּתוֹ	מְדִינָתוֹ	תּוֹרוֹ	◻וֹ	הוּא
יַלְדוּתָהּ	מְדִינָתָהּ	תּוֹרָהּ	◻ָהּ	הִיא
יַלְדוּתֵנוּ	מְדִינָתֵנוּ	תּוֹרֵנוּ	◻ֵנוּ	אָנוּ
יַלְדוּתְכֶם	מְדִינַתְכֶם	תּוֹרְכֶם	◻ְכֶם	אַתֶּם
יַלְדוּתָם	מְדִינָתָם	תּוֹרָם	◻ָם	הֵם

*Note: when the word ends with a ה , the ה is replaced by ת because it is impossible to have a vowel after ה .

Exercising the usage of prepositions

Cover the Hebrew side and say the sentences from English to Hebrew.

Shalom, do you know me?	שָׁלוֹם. אַתָּה מַכִּיר אוֹתִי?
No, I don't know you. Who are you?	לֹא, אֲנִי לֹא מַכִּיר אוֹתְךָ. מִי אַתָּה?
I am the new neighbor.	אֲנִי הַשָּׁכֵן הֶחָדָשׁ.
Where are you? I don't see you.	אֵיפֹה אַתָּה? אֲנִי לֹא רוֹאֶה אוֹתְךָ.
I am here. Do you really not see me?	אֲנִי כָּאן, אַתָּה בֶּאֱמֶת לֹא רוֹאֶה אוֹתִי?
Ah, yes. Now I can see you. Welcome! I am glad to talk to you.	אָה, כֵּן. עַכְשָׁיו אֲנִי יָכוֹל לִרְאוֹת אוֹתְךָ. בָּרוּךְ הַבָּא. אֲנִי שָׂמֵחַ לְדַבֵּר אִתְּךָ.

I love you.	אֲנִי אוֹהֵב אוֹתָךְ.
Do you really love me? Don't you love her?	אַתָּה בֶּאֱמֶת אוֹהֵב אוֹתִי? אַתָּה לֹא אוֹהֵב אוֹתָהּ?

Can you speak louder?	אַתָּה יָכוֹל לְדַבֵּר יוֹתֵר חָזָק?
I don't hear you.	אֲנִי לֹא שׁוֹמַעַת אוֹתְךָ.
He is there. Can't you see him?	הוּא שָׁם, אַתָּה לֹא רוֹאֶה אוֹתוֹ?
I have been looking for you for an hour already! Where are you?	אֲנִי מְחַפֵּשׂ אוֹתְךָ כְּבָר שָׁעָה! אֵיפֹה אַתְּ?
We are taking him to a doctor.	אֲנַחְנוּ לוֹקְחִים אוֹתוֹ לְרוֹפֵא.
Don't you understand me?	אַתְּ לֹא מְבִינָה אוֹתִי?
No, I don't understand you.	לֹא, אֲנִי לֹא מְבִינָה אוֹתְךָ.
I don't understand them, because they speak fast.	אֲנִי לֹא מֵבִין אוֹתָם כִּי הֵם מְדַבְּרִים מַהֵר.
I don't know them.	אֲנִי לֹא מַכִּיר אוֹתָם.
I meet with him every day.	אֲנִי נִפְגָּשׁ אִתּוֹ כָּל יוֹם.
I need to meet with him.	אֲנִי צָרִיךְ לְהִיפָּגֵשׁ אִתּוֹ.
I want to talk with you.	אֲנִי רוֹצָה לְדַבֵּר אִתְּכֶם.
She doesn't like talking to me.	הִיא לֹא אוֹהֶבֶת לְדַבֵּר אִתִּי.
I like studying with her.	אֲנִי אוֹהֵב לִלְמוֹד אִתָּהּ.
They like working with us.	הֵם אוֹהֲבִים לַעֲבוֹד אִתָּנוּ.
Where are Moshe and Chaim, I have been looking for them all morning long and I don't know where they are.	אֵיפֹה מֹשֶׁה וְחַיִּים? אֲנִי מְחַפֵּשׂ אוֹתָם כָּל הַבּוֹקֶר וְלֹא יוֹדֵעַ אֵיפֹה הֵם.

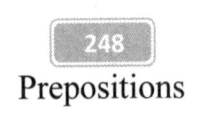

Additional prepositions

And now we are going to look at four additional prepositions that are combined with pronouns. These have a slightly different sound scheme when conjugated. Conjugation of these prepositions is similar to conjugation in plural.

Sons = בָּנִים

(My sons) הַבָּנִים שֶׁלִי = בָּנַי

Pronoun	General structure	To - אֶל	About, On - עַל	After/ Before לִפְנֵי/אַחֲרֵי
אֲנִי	◌ַי	אֵלַי — To me	עָלַי — On me	לְפָנַי / אַחֲרַי
אַתָּה	◌ֶיךָ	אֵלֶיךָ — To you	עָלֶיךָ — On you	לְפָנֶיךָ / אַחֲרֶיךָ
אַתְּ	◌ַיִךְ	אֵלַיִךְ — To you	עָלַיִךְ — On you	לְפָנַיִךְ / אַחֲרַיִךְ
הוּא	◌ָיו	אֵלָיו — To him	עָלָיו — On him	לְפָנָיו / אַחֲרָיו
הִיא	◌ֶיהָ	אֵלֶיהָ — To her	עָלֶיהָ — On her	לְפָנֶיהָ / אַחֲרֶיהָ
אָנוּ	◌ֵינוּ	אֵלֵינוּ — To us	עָלֵינוּ — On us	לְפָנֵינוּ / אַחֲרֵינוּ
אַתֶּם	◌ֵיכֶם	אֲלֵיכֶם — To you (m, plural)	עֲלֵיכֶם — On you (m, plural)	לִפְנֵיכֶם / אַחֲרֵיכֶם
הֵם	◌ֵיהֶם	אֲלֵיהֶם — To them	עֲלֵיהֶם — On them	לִפְנֵיהֶם / אַחֲרֵיהֶם

Examples:

אל	Do you want to call me?	?אתה רוצה לצלצל אלי
	When do you want to come to us?	?מתי אתה רוצה לבוא אלינו
על	Can I trust you?	?אפשר לסמוך עליך
	I thought about you yesterday.	.חשבתי עליכם אתמול

* Note: לצלצל ל.. = to call someone (on the phone),
I called Moshe – צלצלתי למשה
However, when conjugated with a pronoun the preposition ל..
changes to preposition אֶל....

Conjugating nouns in plural

שְׁאֵלָה ← שְׁאֵלוֹת	חָבֵר ← חֲבֵרִים	בֵּן ← בָּנִים	General structure	Pronoun
שְׁאֵלוֹתַי	חֲבֵרַי	בָּנַי	◻ַי	אֲנִי
שְׁאֵלוֹתֶיךָ	חֲבֵרֶיךָ	בָּנֶיךָ	◻ֶיךָ	אַתָּה
שְׁאֵלוֹתַיִךְ	חֲבֵרַיִךְ	בָּנַיִךְ	◻ַיִךְ	אַתְּ
שְׁאֵלוֹתָיו	חֲבֵרָיו	בָּנָיו	◻ָיו	הוּא
שְׁאֵלוֹתֶיהָ	חֲבֵרֶיהָ	בָּנֶיהָ	◻ֶיהָ	הִיא
שְׁאֵלוֹתֵינוּ	חֲבֵרֵינוּ	בָּנֵינוּ	◻ֵינוּ	אָנוּ
שְׁאֵלוֹתֵיכֶם	חבריכם	בְּנֵיכֶם	◻ֵיכֶם	אַתֶּם
שְׁאֵלוֹתֵיהֶן	חבריהם	בְּנֵיהֶם	◻ֵיהֶם	הֵם

Please note that in Hebrew we often use a form which actually has a double affirmation. For example, the sentence "Danni's friends" can be expressed in Hebrew as:

Option 1:   1. הַחֲבֵרִים שֶׁל דָּנִי

Option 2:   2. חֲבֵרָיו שֶׁל דָּנִי

In the second option the word **חֲבֵרָיו** already has the meaning "his friends", so literally the sentence means "His, Danni's friends" affirming Danni's association with friends twice.

Exercise: Translate the following questions (<u>conjugating the nouns</u>) and answer them in Hebrew.

1. Do Miriam's friends visit her?
2. Does the teacher answer our questions?
3. Where do Daniel's sons go on Saturday?
4. Where do your parents visit when they come to Israel?
5. Where do your brothers live?
6. Who takes Rafi's books every morning?

Practice conjugating pronouns

Turn the sentence with nouns into sentences with conjugated pronouns using the examples.

לָגוּר בְּ, עִם

Sentence with a conjugated pronoun	Sentence with a noun
אַתָּה רוֹצֶה לָגוּר בּוֹ? (in it)	אַתָּה רוֹצֶה לָגוּר בַּבַּיִת?
אַתָּה רוֹצֶה לָגוּר אִתּוֹ? (with him)	אַתָּה רוֹצֶה לָגוּר עִם מֹשֶׁה?

לֶאֱכֹל אֶת, בְּ, עִם

Sentence with a conjugated pronoun	Sentence with a noun
הַיּוֹם אֲנִי אוֹכֵל אִתָּם (with them)	הַיּוֹם אֲנִי אוֹכֵל עִם דָּוִיד וּמֹשֶׁה
	הַיּוֹם אֲנִי אוֹכֵל עִם חַנָּה
	אֲנִי אוֹכֵל אֶת הַלֶּחֶם

לָשֶׁבֶת בְּ, עַל, עִם

Sentence with a conjugated pronoun	Sentence with a noun
אֲנִי יוֹשֵׁב עָלָיו	אֲנִי יוֹשֵׁב עַל הַכִּסֵּא (chair) (m)
	אֲנִי יוֹשֵׁב עַל הַסַּפָּה
	אֲנִי יוֹשֵׁב עִם מִיכָאֵל

לָלֶכֶת אֶל

Sentence with a conjugated pronoun	Sentence with a noun
אַתָּה רוֹצֶה לָלֶכֶת אֵלֶיהָ?	אַתָּה רוֹצֶה לָלֶכֶת אֶל חַנָּה הָעֶרֶב?
	אַתָּה הוֹלֵךְ אֶל מֹשֶׁה הַיּוֹם?

לָקַחַת אֶת

Sentence with a conjugated pronoun	Sentence with a noun
אַתְּ רוֹצָה לָקַחַת אוֹתָהּ לַגַּן?	אַתְּ רוֹצָה לָקַחַת אֶת שָׂרָה לַגַּן?
	אַתְּ לוֹקַחַת אֶת הַיְלָדִים לְבֵית הַסֵּפֶר?
	אַתָּה לוֹקֵחַ אֶת הַסֵּפֶר לָעֲבוֹדָה?

Prepositions

לָתֵת ל, אֶת

Sentence with a conjugated pronoun	Sentence with a noun
מָה אַתָּה רוֹצֶה לָתֵת **לוֹ**?	מָה אַתָּה רוֹצֶה לָתֵת לְמֹשֶׁה?
	אַתָּה נוֹתֵן **אֶת** הַסֵּפֶר **לְדִינָה**?
	אֲנִי נוֹתֵן **אֶת** הַפֵּרוֹת **לַיְלָדִים**.

לִרְשֹׁם אֶת, ב

Sentence with a conjugated pronoun	Sentence with a noun
אַתָּה רוֹשֵׁם **אוֹתוֹ**	אַתָּה רוֹשֵׁם **אֶת** הַסִּפּוּר
	אַתָּה רוֹשֵׁם **בַּסֵּפֶר**?

לִזְכֹּר אֶת

Sentence with a conjugated pronoun	Sentence with a noun
אַתָּה זוֹכֵר **אוֹתוֹ**?	אַתָּה זוֹכֵר **אֶת** הַסִּפּוּר?
	אַתְּ זוֹכֶרֶת **אֶת** מִרְיָם?

לִשְׁכֹּחַ אֶת

Sentence with a conjugated pronoun	Sentence with a noun
קַל לִשְׁכֹּחַ **אוֹתָם**?	קַל לִשְׁכֹּחַ **אֶת** הַדְּבָרִים הַטּוֹבִים?
	אַתָּה שׁוֹכֵחַ **אֶת** הַשֵּׁם שֶׁלּוֹ?

לַעֲשׂוֹת אֶת

Sentence with a conjugated pronoun	Sentence with a noun
אַתָּה עוֹשֶׂה **אוֹתָם** בַּבַּיִת?	אַתָּה עוֹשֶׂה **אֶת** הַשִּׁעוּרִים בַּבַּיִת?
	אַתָּה עוֹשֶׂה **אֶת** הָעֲבוֹדָה?

לִקְנוֹת אֶת

Sentence with a conjugated pronoun	Sentence with a noun
אַתְּ קוֹנָה **אוֹתָם** בַּשּׁוּק?	אַתְּ קוֹנָה **אֶת** הַפֵּרוֹת בַּשּׁוּק?
	אַתָּה קוֹנֶה **אֶת** הַקָּפֶה בַּמַּכֹּלֶת?

Prepositions

לְדַבֵּר עִם

Sentence with a conjugated pronoun	Sentence with a noun
אַתֶּם מְדַבְּרִים **אִתָּם** הַיּוֹם?	אַתֶּם מְדַבְּרִים **עִם** הַחֲבֵרִים הַיּוֹם?
	אַתְּ מְדַבֶּרֶת עִם חַנָּה הַיּוֹם?

לְצַלְצֵל לְ, אֶל

Sentence with a conjugated pronoun	Sentence with a noun
אַתָּה צָרִיךְ לְצַלְצֵל **אֲלֵיהֶם** הַיּוֹם?	אַתָּה צָרִיךְ לְצַלְצֵל **לַ**הוֹרִים שֶׁלְּךָ הַיּוֹם?
	אַתֶּם מְצַלְצְלִים **לְ**מֹשֶׁה הַיּוֹם?

לְבַשֵּׁל אֶת

Sentence with a conjugated pronoun	Sentence with a noun
אַתָּה רוֹצֶה לְבַשֵּׁל **אוֹתוֹ** לַאֲרוּחַת הָעֶרֶב?	אַתָּה רוֹצֶה לְבַשֵּׁל **אֶת** הַבָּשָׂר לַאֲרוּחַת הָעֶרֶב?
	אַתְּ צְרִיכָה לְבַשֵּׁל **אֶת** הַיְרָקוֹת.

לְנַקּוֹת אֶת

Sentence with a conjugated pronoun	Sentence with a noun
אַתָּה אוֹהֵב לְנַקּוֹת **אוֹתוֹ**?	אַתָּה אוֹהֵב לְנַקּוֹת **אֶת** הַבַּיִת?
	אַתְּ אוֹהֶבֶת לְנַקּוֹת **אֶת** הַדִּירָה?

לְהָבִין אֶת

Sentence with a conjugated pronoun	Sentence with a noun
אֲנִי לֹא מֵבִין **אוֹתוֹ**.	אֲנִי לֹא מֵבִין **אֶת** הַמּוֹרָה.
	אַתְּ מְבִינָה **אֶת** הַיְלָדִים?

Summary Exercise

Translate the following.

Where are your (pl.) friends?	
Is this yours? (sing., m.)	
Do you have (pl.) coffee?	
I am just telling you (sing., f.) what I think.	
Your (sing., f.) house is really pretty.	
I love you (sing., m.)	
I can't hear you (sing., m.).	
Are you (sing., m.) traveling with them to Eilat?	
Are you (sing., f.) with her today?	
What are you (sing., m.) studying with them?	
Are you (sing., m.) eating with him in the restaurant today?	
Are you (sing., f.) praying with her on Shabbat?	
Is this letter from her?	
Are you (sing., m.) writing the book on your own?	